Devas and Nature Spirits

AND HOW TO COMMUNICATE WITH THEM

KATHLEEN PEPPER

with illustrations by Patrick Gamble & Bodel Rikys

Polair Publishing
LONDON

First Published by Polair Publishing, London, September 2019

© Kathleen Pepper 2019
Illustrations © Patrick Gamble, 2019 and Bodel Rikys, 2019.

British Library Cataloguing in Publication Data
A Catalogue Record for this book is obtainable from the British Library
ISBN 978-1-905398-52-2

DEDICATION

I should like to dedicate this book to my son Nigel who has beeen a tower of strength to me in the creation of this book. Thank you, Nigel, for your patience in helping me with computing.

ACKNOWLEDGMENTS

First of all, I should like to thank Colum Hayward of Polair Publishing for his helpful support, patience, editing and advice. I should like to thank Patrick Gamble and Bodel Rikys for their illustrations. The White Eagle Lodge, both at New Lands and in London has been with me throughout, and I am grateful to the White Eagle Lodge for permission to use the quotations from White Eagle, which are © Copyright, The White Eagle Lodge. White Eagle books are available from whiteagle.org.
Sharry has introduced me to many fairy friends; Alison Knox of everdayangelsart.com has given support and encouragement, and Jo and Dom de Rosa of innerguidance.co.uk have shared with me their beautiful centre, their fairy garden and thier support of the natural world. Lesley, Meher, Thrity and Anna have given support through challenging times. I'd also like to thank Elyan Stephens and the Bro Dyfi White Eagle Centre in Wales, and all my friends who have read my newsletters, attended my workshops and shared their ideas.

Printed in Great Britain by the Halstan Printing Group, Amersham

CONTENTS

SECTION ONE
Developing your Visionary Powers

MESSAGE FROM FAIRIES, THE FAIR FOLK

Even our name is fair,
Indicating justice and beauty,
Both meanings found in the word 'fair.'
So we are fairies.
We are everywhere in your world, but we are not three-dimensional.
You will find us 'between' dimensions in the fair(y) places of the world.
We love beauty
And will enhance even the plants you call weeds
And the wildflowers of derelict areas, for without us, indeed,
Nothing will grow.
We honour those who do their best to conserve the gifts of Mother Earth (Gaia).
We abhor waste.
If you co-operate with us, the earth will be saved.,
And become FAIR again.
We will give ideas to those who seek new means of energy.
These ideas are just around the corner,
Or 'between the dimensions'.
Dream them into reality.

Chapter One

LEARN TO SEE DEVAS, ANGELS, NATURE SPIRITS AND FAIRIES

DEVAS, elementals and nature spirits are all around us. They each have their particular role. It is said that each blade of grass, each leaf on a tree and even each grain of sand on the seashore has its own fairy or deva. If we could all see with our inner vision and if we developed our intuitive gifts, we would be amazed at the variety of spiritual beings that surrounds us.

One of the most effective ways to begin to develop your visionary powers, or inner vision, is through the practice of mindfulness. How many times during the day do you find yourself thinking idly, daydreaming or worrying while doing something else, such as the washing up? Being mindful can be practised at any suitable time in your day and doing any activity. You can spend just five minutes at a time observing what you are doing. It can begin when you first wake up in the morning. Choose one thing to do at a time and spend five minutes or so with mindful moments.

So, right away, let's have some exercises.

BEGINNING THE DAY

WAKING UP

Notice your feelings as you wake up – lazy, tired, keen to get up and go or not, excited or depressed at what the day ahead has in store.

Begin to stretch and breathe, and then breathe more deeply.

Notice how you begin to wake up as you breathe and stretch.

IN THE SHOWER

Feel the water sprinkling over your body and splashing into the shower or bath.

Notice the temperature of the water – cool, maybe even cold, or hot, warm, skin-tingling, soothing, refreshing – waking you up.

Listen to the sound of the water as it falls around

you and feel the drops running off your hair and skin.

BREAKFAST

Be very aware of tastes and textures of the food and drink you are having.

Notice the temperature of the drink.

Feel how it swirls around your mouth and goes down your throat.

Feel the texture of the food you eat as it softens. Chew slowly, feeling the taste as it is released into your taste buds, and then notice how it feels as you swallow.

DURING THE DAY

MINDFUL BREATHING

Allow about five minutes for this – less if you are in a hurry.

Close your eyes and sit in a straight-backed chair and allow your shoulders to roll back and relax. Lift your chest and ribcage but don't tighten them. Close your eyes and begin to breathe slowly and gently. Notice only the breath as it comes and goes. Feel the breath as it enters the nostrils and goes down the throat. Feel the ribs move out, followed by the navel, as the breath pushes into the diaphragm. Don't hold the breath but notice the feeling of wanting to breathe out. Notice the navel fall and the ribs and chest move in again.

Continue to do this as long as you can. Make sure you don't strain. If you find yourself thinking of other things, bring your mind back to the breath. To finish, bring your thoughts to the sounds you can hear and bring your thoughts back to the present.

If you feel tired after a time at work, or during a break, find a safe place to sit outside like a park bench or garden. Then breathe mindfully to revive your energy.

MINDFUL WALKING

Mindful walking can be done at any time of day. You can do it anywhere, going to the office or along the street, along a corridor or a station platform. Notice each footstep as you place the foot on the ground or floor, then notice it as you lift it off – and repeat with the other foot.

SITTING MINDFULLY

Sit in a comfortable straight-backed chair or in the easy cross-legged pose on the floor. Adjust your body so you don't need to move.

Imagine you are like a stone statue, immovable. Be completely aware of your body. If there are any aches or pains, focus on them and nothing else.

Notice any sensation of taste or the feel of saliva in your mouth.

Notice the softness and smoothness of your breath at the tip of the nose. Be aware of any scent or perfume.

Feel the points of contact between your eyelids.

Allow your sense of hearing to range around the room, then outside the building, and notice any sounds.

After some time, allow your mind to travel around your body. Begin at the right foot, then go to the left foot. Notice any sensations in them. Then move on to the right leg, left leg, abdomen, chest, right arm, left arm, neck and head, then the whole body. Tell yourself, 'I will not move my body.'

This is one round. Repeat another round. Five or ten minutes is refreshing in itself. Do it for however long you have available and make sure you are comfortable.

LOOK FOR BEAUTY

A message from the Fairies and Nature Spirits

Look for beauty. Create beauty around you. Make everything you do as beautiful as you can – your home, your garden, your work space. Then we can contact you more easily. People who love beauty will be attracted to you, for they seek beauty, peace and tranquillity. Then a large community of devas and nature spirits who work with beauty are attracted to the area. People begin to experience a refreshing energy that restores harmony in their environment. Above all, the important thing is a pure loving heart, for there is only Love. LOVE brings WISDOM and POWER.

It is also helpful to open your inner vision through your way of living. Healthy eating, enjoyable exercise, if possible in the fresh air, all build strength, health and stamina in the physical body, help you to become more cheerful and less depressed, and help to bring more confidence. Be observant with what happens in the natural world around you. See if there are interesting stones and pebbles on the ground. Just on my garden path I found a small stone with a heart clearly visible on one side. Notice the way leaves and plants move and wave in the breeze. Listen to the sound of the breeze or the falling rain, feel the temperature on your skin, notice the pattern of the clouds in the sky. Lean against trees and feel their energy. Watch the clouds in the sky and notice their shapes and movement.

My husband, Roy, being a research scientist and of a logical train of mind, was always a bit of a sceptic about the things I have been teaching for over forty years. Yet a few weeks before his final illness, we were in the garden and he called me to look at the sky. 'Look,' he said. 'That cloud is just like an angel!' And it was, so I got out my phone to take a photo. In an instant, that particular cloud disappeared, but he had seen it and was cheered by it. All the other clouds were still there, only the angel one had disappeared. He was the scientist and I like to think I am the mystic!

DEVELOPING IMAGINATION

We could all see with our inner vision if we practised using it. Unfortunately we dismiss this gift of human ability as imagination. It is true that some people have a natural gift to see into the spiritual life behind every aspect of creation, but we can all develop the gift through practice.

The first step is to practise using it – the imagination. The education that we all go through really only develops one aspect of the brain. Often referred to as the left brain, this is used for logical thinking, analysis and mathematical processes. The right brain is the part of us that uses visualization, imagery, and all things creative.[1] About forty years ago, a popular book that came to the fore was DRAWING ON THE RIGHT SIDE OF THE BRAIN by Dr Betty Edwards, an art educator. The first edition was published in 1979 and an expanded and updated edition in 1999. She found some research in 1968 by psychobiologist Roger W. Sperry on human brain hemisphere functions.[2] He gained a Nobel Prize for his work.

Sperry discovered that the human brain uses two fundamentally different modes of thinking. One is verbal, analytic and sequential and one is visual and perceptual. Edwards's book was aimed at budding artists, including those who lacked confidence in their drawing ability because of embarrassment due to early schooling, when they were told they couldn't draw. I read it avidly, having always been keen on any art projects.

About the same time I also read THE CREATIVE JOURNAL: THE ART OF FINDING YOURSELF by Dr Lucia Capacchione, a registered art therapist. It made the point that if you write and draw with the non-dominant hand (usually it is the left hand but if you are left-handed, then it is the right) you have a direct link with the creative aspect of yourself. Another useful book by Capacchione was THE POWER OF YOUR OTHER HAND: A COURSE IN CHANNELING THE INNER WISDOM OF THE RIGHT BRAIN, and it was one I used and loved.

I started to draw and write with my left (non-dominant hand). I did this during my time of studying for my Master's Degree in Education from 1987 to 1992. I also had a full-time career so it was a time of great pressure for me. I have always been clairvoyant but decided that academic study was preventing me from being creative. To my amazement, I wrote my first poem in 1990 and I produced several journals writing and drawing with my left hand. From that experience have developed all the poems and meditations in this present book and my other ones.

In fact, this theory about the brain is somewhat

outdated by more recent research: over the years there have been a lot of scientific investigations into the way the brain functions. They have shown that there are more ways of studying the brain than there were sixty years ago and the distinction between the left and the right brain is more complicated than was once thought.[1]

Through practice we can extend our ability to develop clairvoyance or inner vision. Clairvoyance, clear seeing, is not the only spiritual gift. There are five intuitive senses altogether: clairaudience, clear hearing; clairsentience, inner feelings; claircognizance, inner knowing; and clairailence, clear smelling. So what *are* these intuitive and spiritual gifts?

As with all psychic and spiritual experiences, it is very important to be clear about what the visualizations you have might mean. Don't allow yourself to be carried away by imagination to do crazy things. Wait and more guidance may follow that confirms or denies the experience. Often the same guidance may follow in three different ways, but wait before rushing to act on it.

Clairvoyance

You may see more things than happen in the physical world. Usually clairvoyance manifests as images in the mind, whence comes the word *imagination*. This is what is known as the *third eye*. Some people see things in colour, others in black and white, or even both at different times. You might see symbols, colours, patterns, numbers or names.

Meditation is an ideal way to develop inner vision and learn to interpret the signs and symbols you get. Some people say they can't visualize. A good beginning is to imagine an orange. Create the picture of an orange in your mind's eye. You can do this from memory. Develop the feeling of the orange in your hand. Feel the texture of its skin. Imagine digging your thumb into the peel. Imagine the scent of the orange as its juice spurts out. Peel the orange. Feel its juice on your fingers. Take a segment and put it in your mouth. Feel the sensation and taste of the juice. Saliva pours into your mouth.

All this can be done from memory, as it's something you have probably done many times. This is the beginning of visualization. Like everything, practice makes perfect.

You may be clairvoyant if you:
• Have vivid dreams
• Daydream a lot
• Can see colours, shapes, symbols or pictures when you close your eyes
• See sparkly light, flashes of light or

movements out of the corners of your eyes.

If you are clairvoyant, your preferred phrase in acknowledging what others have said is 'I see'.

Here is an account from a healer called Kay. She calls it 'a phenomenal experience'.

'A few years ago my sister and I had a wonderful phenomenal experience. We were sitting in her lounge looking out at a common alder tree in her garden. To our amazement the tree suddenly became alive with little white lights, followed by a covering of golden lights. It was as if a huge firework of gold and white energy had covered the entire tree. This went on for at least ten minutes after which it started to gradually fade away. We quickly realized that all trees must have the same phenomenal energy. We felt privileged to see it.'

Clairaudience

You can hear messages, usually inside your mind. It is a form of telepathy used to communicate with spiritual beings. You can speak to spirits mentally and they can reply. Sometimes it sounds like your own voice, except you can be surprised by what you hear. It's often something you don't know. Many clairaudients think they have nagging thoughts or maybe crazy ideas that just pop into their minds.

They can tell somebody something but they don't know how they know it. Clairaudients often talk to themselves. Usually the messages or conversations they hear are either in the left or right ear. A buzzing or humming sound can be detected in the predominant ear. Clairaudient thoughts are heard from the back of the head, while personal thoughts originate from the front part of the head.

A few years ago I was on a spiritual retreat on the Island of Iona in the Hebrides. A group of us were walking across the island to a beautiful beach. I felt very in tune with nature, the soft breeze, warm sunshine, the sound of the sea and sea birds. Iona has traditionally been associated with the ancient civilization of Atlantis because of a green and white marble-like stone found there. Suddenly I heard a voice in my right ear.

'Soon you will be on the shore of our beloved Atlantis.'

I felt very happy, as though ancient happy memories were stirring in my soul.

If you are clairaudient you may:
• Listen more than talk
• Talk to animals or plants and hear them reply.

If you are clairaudient, your preferred phrase when acknowledging what others have said is 'I hear'.

Clairsentience

This is the ability to feel strongly, beyond the physical. Such people feel or sense the emotions of others and of animals, spirit beings and places around them. Sometimes these people are called 'empaths'.

Once my family were going to picnic on a beach. My mother and I were in front, my husband and small child behind. It was a beautiful beach, with lovely smooth sand and deserted. When we got onto the beach, my mother and I turned round and walked away again, saying we can't possibly go there. My husband was mystified! Later, we discovered there had been a massacre there several centuries before. My mother and I had picked up the vibrations of ancient energy.

A similar thing happened to a friend who lived in Texas. He couldn't bear to go into the Alamo, near San Antonio. When I visited, I too felt the violence and fear that had been experienced there.

In some ways clairsentience is a more difficult gift, as people don't understand why they have the feelings they do. They are experienced as their own feelings. Such people are very compassionate and understanding towards others.

If you are clairsentient you:
- May be highly sensitive to the places you go to and to your surroundings.
- May feel unhappy in crowds, with unexplained emotional or physical reactions
- Can sometimes feel other people's pain in your body, even its location in their body
- Find that your feelings change when you visit others or their homes
- Your preferred phrase when acknowledging what others have said is 'I feel'.

Claircognizance

You just know information, even if you don't know how you know it. The knowledge comes spontaneously. It might be facts and figures or simply knowing the truth of a situation.
You may be claircognizant:

If you get answers and information from 'nowhere'.

Your mind is like a butterfly, always swirling from one idea to the next, especially if you are working on a creative project.

You 'just know' if someone is telling the truth or giving true information.

Clairailence

This is the ability to pick up information through scents and smells, such as perfume or tobacco smoke, when there isn't anything there. You may be clairailent if:
•   You have strong memories triggered by scents and smells
•   You are very sensitive to scents and smells, which can repel or attract you
•   You like to surround yourself with good scents like essential oils, incense and perfume.

You may have a combination of any or all of the above spiritual gifts and regular meditation will train you to be able to use them. These are invaluable ways of attuning to the natural world, to devas, elementals and angels.

LEARN TO EXPERIENCE THE PRESENCE OF DEVAS AND ELEMENTALS

Many people refer to seeing fairies, devas and elementals but, as we saw above, seeing (clairvoyance) is only one way of experiencing them. The very best way of training yourself to see them is to practise daily meditation or mindfulness.

   A useful way of opening the 'imagination' is doodling and drawing. As we now live in a time when people feel stressed, there has been a recent enthusiasm for more simple ways to relax and let go. There is a vast range of creative books that can be bought in any bookseller or even a supermarket, as well as the internet. You can find books that encourage adult colouring, or doodling and moving on to more advanced projects such as Zen Tangle Art and Zen Doodling.[1] Here is a simple exercise to begin to unlock your creativity and ability to see and experience different dimensions.

TAKING PENCILS FOR A WALK

Take three different coloured pencils and a piece of A4 paper or use an A4 drawing book (or US letter size). In fact, the bigger the better, as it allows for freer movement of your hand.

Start to scribble on the paper. Draw shapes and patterns in all directions, just allow your hand to fly over the paper. Use both hands if you want to. Cover the paper and when you have finished put it to one side. Allow your mind to relax.

Sometime later start to gaze at your drawing. Gaze rather than look hard. Try looking cross-eyed at it if you can or look out of the sides of your eyes. If you wear glasses you could take them off. You can do this more than once. Then suddenly you might see patterns or symbols that you didn't intentionally put there.

Try to interpret what you see, as this is training your eyes to look at things differently from the way you look at everyday objects or documents. There are workbooks available now which deal with doodling and drawing.. See the notes at the back of this book for details.[1]

PAINTING

Recently I went to an acrylic painting weekend. I'll write more about it shortly, but the subject was 'Paint Your Healing Tree'. I was shown how to prepare the background for the painting using different colours of paint and sponges to rub the wet paint around to create an interesting background. We were concentrating on the sky and foreground, before even going on to the rest.

When I had finished I was astonished to see that there were angels and elementals in the sky and grass. I hadn't put them there intentionally. It could be a form of channeling or automatic painting. It is a way that the spiritual world can contact you.

PAINTING ACTIVITY

If you have any paints, experiment with mixing and blending different colours and shades to see what happens. A child's watercolour paintbox will be suitable if you don't have your own paints. You can mix them onto a sheet of plain paper and play around with making different results.

When you want to paint a tree trunk, consider how many colours can make up brown. If painting grass, what colours would blend together into green to make interesting shadows and shades? When you paint sea or sky, what colours blend with blue to make it interesting? If you are up at dawn or sunset, look at the sky and notice how the colours change from moment to moment. Experiment with blending the colours you see.

BEING AWARE OF COLOUR

Focusing on colour is a magnificent route to healing and helping you to attune to nature, elementals, fairies and devas. For a start, the natural world is full of colour. Artists often blend colours in an imaginative way as they have learned the art of blending paint colours.

Devas, fairies and elementals adore colour. Every flower and plant is full of colour and in more than one shade. Many people have to wear sober colours in their professional life but colour can be introduced in subtle ways using jewellery, nail polish, socks, shirts and ties.

Try to become more aware of colours in the world around you. If you live or work in a city, notice colourful posters and adverts. Make an effort to visit a garden in your lunch hour or before or after work if you can. Many buildings now display beautiful flower arrangements in hanging baskets. My local tube station has a keen gardener on the staff who grows flowers and herbs in plant boxes along the platform. If you travel by train or bus, look out of the window and notice the plants that grow alongside the road or embankment. As well as enabling you to enjoy the scenery, the plants and trees on the banks are a haven for wildlife and exactly the kind of places that the devas, fairies and elementals can best enjoy their work.

In this technological age, try to become more aware of the natural world rather than spending time on a smartphone, tablet or computer. These technologies, useful though they are, cut us off from what we can attune to around us. The more you can notice and observe what happens around you, the more your clairvoyant and other spiritual gifts will open and develop. In fact, some of the spiritual teachers recommend us to do that to open our spiritual gifts.

I love visiting gardens in the summer when all the flowers are blooming. Each plant has its own deva and every flower has a fairy that cares for it. The colours of the flowers can also be meaningful. The seven main energy centres (chakras) resonate with colours. I have included some photographs of flowers that I have taken as an example to help you.

■ **Red** – be grounded and firm, find courage and strength.

Another message of red is gratitude.

■ **Orange** – be creative. Write or draw, visit a beautiful place or an art gallery.

Yellow – Use more light or use your spiritual wisdom, find your own favourite method of being creative and practise it every day or whenever you can.

Green is the colour of the heart chakra. It assists us to be adaptable and harmonious. It is a colour of trust. Walking in a park or woodland helps to develop trust.

Blue is the colour of the throat chakra. Work with helpful affirmations or mantras that help you gain positivity and confidence.

Indigo is the colour of the third eye or eyebrow centre. You might think of it as the mind's eye. It helps to develop your intuition. Start to follow your hunches in simple ways and see if they are true.

Violet is the colour of the crown chakra, at the top of the head. It connects with the higher self or spirit You can use what is

called the Violet Flame to cleanse yourself and work with your higher self.

Visualize yourself being surrounded and filled with the colour you see. Other useful colours that you can use to develop your spiritual gifts are pink and white.

Pink is the colour of the palm of the hand and another colour that relates to the heart chakra. The hands are used in service to others in the ways that we help friends and family in the way we care for them. Hands are creative and we use our hands for everything we do.

White is the colour of spirit. It contains all the colours of the spectrum.

CONNECTING TO DEVAS AND NATURE SPIRITS

The plants and rocks all have angel guardians, as well as elementals, or tiny sprites or beings of light. These act rather like the spirit guide of a person but to a plant, crystal or rock or other living being. When you are out in the country, in the mountains, or by the ocean, notice the energy and purity of the atmosphere. Find somewhere to sit quietly and feel as if you are a part of the natural scenery. Breathe in the pure fresh air and notice it filling your body. Tune in to your breath. Notice how refreshed you start to feel.

Visualize yourself surrounded by pure white light. The white light reflects gold and silver light and the colours of the natural world that surround you. Continue to focus on your breath and the colours until you are filled with light and colour. Take the light and colour into your heart chakra.

Then look around you. You may notice tiny sparks or flashes of light, colour or orbs, which are how elementals and fairies may show themselves. Sometimes these will appear on a photo, so take some random photos of different scenes and look for lights and images that are only visible on the photo. You may be able to visualize elementals and fairies with your eyes closed, your inner vision. Again don't tell yourself it's your imagination.

Continue to follow your breath and go deeper. Think of nothing else except your breathing and the scene where you are sitting. Go deeper and notice what you experience. How do you feel? Are you hot or cold? Do you feel a tingling sensation in your hands and feet? Are you aware of colours or symbols? Do you mentally hear a voice or message? These are some of the ways you may be aware of elementals. Keep your awareness on your breathing and gaze around you. Do you notice an 'aura' of light or colour around the plants, trees or scenery? If you do, you have successfully contacted the elemental kingdom.

Iris is the deva of colour and flower fairies. She was the Greek goddess of the rainbow. The different colours of the iris show the colour of the rainbow itself. The iris flower fairies can open your vision to the fairy kingdom. They can give great inspiration and inspire creativity. They can bring about a sense of peace and hope for new birth.[1]

The artist Vincent van Gogh painted several pictures of irises, each of which is unique. He studied the movement of the flowers and petals and painted a variety of wavy, curling and twisting shapes.

Wikimedia Commons (Public Domain)

DEVAS – GUARDIANS OF THE LAND

Wherever you go, there will be a number of devas who are guardians of the land. They are like spirit guides for the plants and trees and you can become aware of them when you have trained your abilities to communicate with the natural world.

On the summer solstice I decided to go for an early morning walk in my local nature area. Suddenly it was as if my inner vision had opened more. I think of it as an 'a-ha' moment. There is a creaky old gated entrance with wire mesh fencing. The gate has been there ever since I moved to the area nearly forty years ago, when the land was disused allotments. With my inner vision I suddenly 'saw' the gate with two beings standing guard at the entrance. I greeted them as guardians of the gate, guardians of love, wisdom and protection of that nature area I do this mentally now whenever I go in and out of the gate.

As I walked around the area, I suddenly became aware of the four directions – East, South, West, and North. I tuned in to the trees that seemed to be the guardians of each direction.

East is the place of the sunrise and the time of new beginnings. A young oak tree was there. In time it would grow to a great size but now it was young, full of potential of strength and courage. Its

Rowan trees (mountain ash) are renowned for protection against negative energies and elder are well known for being magical. I consider these to be guardians of the land they grow on.

A MESSAGE FROM THE DEVAS

Our messages come to you
In simple subtle ways,
And not always in words.
We are in the sound of the softly falling rain,
The sweet songs of the birds,
The scent of the flowers,
The gentle touch of the soft breezes blowing around you,
The laughter of children,
The kindness of family and friends,
The smile of a stranger in the street or the store.
We are in the 'good luck' that comes your way
In numerous synchronicities.
We are in the music you hear
And the books you suddenly or mysteriously find
On a shelf in a bookshop or library.
YES!!!
Live joyfully so your life is filled with enjoyment,
For Joy is meant.
Live in thanks so your life is filled with thankfulness.
Live hopefully so your life is filled with Hope.
Our message today is
TRUST
And within that word is US.

essence is one of the Bach flower remedies that can be taken for strength, courage and endurance (see p. 43). In the Celtic tradition of the British Isles, oak is king of the woods and ruled by the planet Jupiter.

The white eagle (white denoting a spiritual being) is the guardian of the East. Eagle also represents courage and the opportunity to fly high above the clouds of every day concerns and challenges to reach divine inspiration.

Walking clockwise (sunwise) I came to the South, the place of the summer sun, warmth and the innocence of the inner child. A large rowan tree (mountain ash) tree stands there. It provides shelter for many birds which were very active while I was there. Its Celtic message means 'bright spirit' and represents the fires of Inspiration. The Celtic goddess Brighid is its ruler. South is the place of the white wolf, which is the teacher of the medicine circle and reminds us to work cooperatively and honour children as well as our own inner child.

Walking along the path, at the west I came to a pair of hawthorn trees, one on each side of the path. Thorn trees are known as fairy trees.

At the West were apple trees. The apple tree is known as the tree of life and renowned for giving health and vitality. Its ruler is Iduna. She is the goddess associated with apples and youth. The west is the place of the white bear, denoting the place of 'going within' in meditation to seek goals and make plans. In the autumn, the bear hibernates and gives birth to her cubs, just as we give birth to our plans and goals by going within to meditate.

The North is the place of the ancestors, who gave us life through many generations and still watch over us and help us. It is the place of the white buffalo, the Native American Mother Goddess, who provides abundance for which we pray and give gratitude.

At the North, on each side of the path, were bushes of wild roses of different colours and strong perfume. Rose water has many healing properties and is useful as a skin rejuvenator and mild antiseptic. A Bach flower remedy is made from the wild rose. It is good for people who lack interest in life and are resigned to everything that happens. Roses are recognized as the tree of love for matters of the heart and for partnership. Venus rules the rose and it is said that aeons ago, roses were brought to Planet Earth from Venus.*

So ended my journey around the mysterious Medicine Wheel or circle, which lies behind my house and where I have lived for nearly forty years without recognizing all the spiritual helpers who surround me.

DEVAS AND ANGELS OF CREATION

We are always with you.
Call on us and we are there.
When you tell people about us we are there.
When you call on us
We surround you
Like the petals of a flower,
With all the colours of the rainbow.
Red for the love within the heart of the rose,
Orange for a dancing, flickering magical flame of light,
Yellow for the warmth and upliftment of the sun,
Green for the harmony and refreshment of a summer meadow,
Blue for the serenity and tranquillity of a summer sky,
Indigo for the restfulness of the deepening sky at dusk,
Violet for the sweet scent of spring violets,
Pure white for clarity.
Always we are there, with you,
Around you and within you
In the realms of the natural world.
We are the Angels of Creation
We are the Devas.

Seek us in the green fields and majestic forests,
The soaring snow-capped mountains,

The bubbling streams and the fast flowing river,
The waterfalls and torrents,
And the swiftly falling rain that refreshes the parched earth
Bringing new growth, food for living beings.
Seek us in the burning sand of the deserts
And the raging ocean storms that calm in an instant
To the soft smoothness of the sea that mirrors
The blue sky and floating clouds above.
You will find us everywhere.
We are the Angels of Creation.
We are the Devas.

We send you living streams of Light
Across The Universe
Which are gathered up by Angels, Devas and Nature Spirits
And then transmitted to all of Nature
For health and growth.
We are only a thought away
Always ready to listen to you and surround you
With these living streams of Light
For your sustenance.
Call on us and we are always there
The Angels of Creation
And the Devas.

The Forest of Healing Trees

As I've said, I went to an art workshop with Patrick Gamble, who has contributed illustrations for this book. Their titles are given at the end (p. 102). The workshop was entitled 'The Visionary Artist' and the challenge was to paint your own healing tree. The workshop took place in the New Forest in Hampshire. It gave me a much greater insight into the use of colour in painting.

There was quite a large group of us, all painting a healing tree. After the first day of the workshop I went back to the guesthouse where I was staying and lay down to relax. Suddenly I went into a spontaneous visualization. I was in an old type of manor house with dark panelling on the walls and dark wooden stairs. I was climbing the stairs with a group of people whom I didn't recognize but there were quite a few of us. At the top of the stairs we walked along a dark corridor towards a large room. I told the others that we would be in an art gallery with all the pictures we were painting. However, when we reached the room it disappeared and we were in an actual forest of healing trees.

All the people who had ever been to Patrick's workshops painting healing trees had a tree in that healing forest. The trees were sending out healing to everyone who needed healing and loved to walk amongst the healing energy of trees.

The forest of healing trees is in the world of light, the spirit world. If you want to go there in your meditations to get healing, create the vision of a beautiful forest. If you prefer, you can focus on a picture or some mood music to help with the imagery.

This is also an important meditation to heal the forest itself as the New Forest was established by William the Conqueror for the hunting of animals such as deer and wild boar. Then at the time of the English Civil War many atrocities were committed. At this time, however, people are becoming more aware of planetary healing and the health of Gaia, the goddess of planet Earth.

CLIMATE CHANGE

More and more people are concerned about the state of the planet. People worry about pollution, global warming and violence and other threats and challenges, and rightly so. Organizations and groups are formed to help the situation. One thing is lacking however, in this consternation about the issues at stake. Only a few groups or people are involved with working directly with the nature kingdom – that is, the devas, nature spirits and elementals, angels and archangels who are the energy beneath, within and around all that we see in the beauty of the natural world. Some sensitive people have the gift of experiencing or seeing these beings and are learning to work directly with them in partnership. We can too.

Such a partnership was established in the 1960s at the Findhorn Community in Scotland, which began as an experiment to discover how nature spirits (elementals), angels and human beings could co-operate and work together. This resulted in amazing crops grown in a previously barren area of land. It resulted in a process that was recommended.

This included a recognition that nature spirits (elementals and devas) do exist and need love and thanks from people. Nature is the living world. It's time that we reconnected with nature and learned to reconnect and live in harmony, to honour its life as indigenous people of old did. They knew how to respect the earth and her gifts.

Through the power of thought, their help can be requested. We need to know that they are there and we can speak to them silently or aloud, thanking them for their help.

We need to pay close attention to our intuitive thoughts and feelings and should not dismiss them as imagination. Their guidance is likely to come as a feeling of inner knowing about what to do, a gut feeling as some people might call it. Notice what works and what doesn't and always work with what is successful.

Always lovingly thank the nature spirits and angels.

The other important aspect of this partnership is to create beauty and harmony as much as possible in our own environment, in our homes and workspaces. This makes it possible for nature spirits, fairies, elementals and angels to come near to work with us.

GARDENS

Gardens are important to the planet. For every garden there is a deva who is the guardian of that part of the land and elementals who work with it to enhance the health and beauty of the plants. This healing energy also influences and improves the health of the area. The United Kingdom seems to be a land of beautiful gardens and they bring spiritual energy to the area. People can cooperate with the elementals and devas and bring new life to the vegetables, just as was done at Findhorn. For all our love of gardens many are being lost to tarmac and concrete in our towns, everywhere, yet plants are the lungs of the earth and also bring peace and tranquillity to those who love nature.

For every beautiful and well-kept garden there is a guardian of the land, a deva who directs the fairies and elemental beings and holds the mental 'blueprint' for the area. They work there to enhance the health and beauty of the plants and in turn this enhances the health of the area.

Elves work with the guardian. They are about the size of a young teenager, a youth or young girl who is beautiful to see. Sit quietly in your garden, breathing quietly. You may see the elves or guardian at work in that place. The elves work particularly with the flowers and will be wearing the colours

The Devas' Message about Gardens

We want to tell you how important gardens are. The world is being concreted over – but plants are the wings and lungs of the earth. A garden brings to life more than just the plants you see. A garden is a portal of light for the whole environment. It is more of a nature conservation area.

Everyone who loves the plants in their gardens encourages the fairies and elementals to bring new life to the plants and even to each grain of soil. The design of a garden is a form of creativity and inspiration. Plants and beautiful design inspire visitors with colours and fragrances. People receive the gift of peace and tranquillity and take ideas and inspiration back to their own gardens.

'Look for hidden patterns and shapes in the petals or leaves that indicate a fairy or nature spirit'
Patterns of light on a tree trunk; a trunk full of stories; mysterious light on the garden fence

of the flowers that they care for and that are in season. Sometimes they can be seen as orbs or coloured lights in digital photos.

In the garden look for hidden patterns and shapes in the petals or leaves that indicate a fairy or nature spirit (see above for some examples). They attract the people who work there with the beauty of plants and the design of the garden or park. These nature spirits and devas send out healing energy and light to the immediate environment. They will cooperate with anybody who is attuned to the spiritual energies. Birds and insects are attracted to the plants they need for homes and food and people can sit on a warm sunny day to listen to the song of the birds and the hum of the bees. Even one loved garden in an urban street is a source of important spiritual beauty and improves the quality of life for the inhabitants.

The cooperation between human beings and the elementals at the Findhorn Community was an example of the partnership between devas, angels and people. While Findhorn is in a mainly rural and coastal area, it is equally important to build cooperation and communication in the great cities of the world. Each apparently small community touches the whole area and the spiritual healing energy continues for many years.

IDEAS TO DRAW IN DEVAS, ANGELS AND ELEMENTALS

- When planting new plants, bring healing energy either to the plant or the area of planting, using prayer or attunement.
- Create a sacred circle in the area. If it is in a large area the energy will circulate and create a focus for meetings. Use stones and crystals from places you visit.
- Plant healing herbs
- Create a circle of flowers of the colours of the directions.
- Burn sacred smudge (white sage or bundles of sweet scented herbs specially prepared) in each corner of the garden or area.

In addition:
- line garden paths with crystals and rose quartz tumble stones so people can walk along a path symbolizing love and cooperation.
- the entrance to the property can have a quartz crystal on each side of the gate to cleanse and energize visitors, offer protection and act as guardians. Small crystals can be buried in the ground or hidden out of sight if necessary.
- A small community of like-minded people can come together and begin to use the ideas in their own homes so the light and healing energy spreads.

DEVAS AND ANGELS OF CREATION

The partnership between angels, archangels, devas and humans is an ancient contract, which was established at the dawn of time itself. According to ancient scriptures, when God created human beings he said, 'They will be like us' (Genesis 1 : 26), which implies that the Creator, the Source of All That Is, had companions. Probably they were angels, often referred to as Elohim.

Another name for angels is shining ones (devas) or light beings. The angels of creation were created to assist God in the creation of the universe. In Psalm 148, we read:

'Shout praises to the Lord!
Shout the Lord's praises in the highest heavens.
All you angels, and all who serve him above
Come and offer praise.'

Some Jewish writings and other traditions assert that angels were each created every morning from the breath of God, so angels are sometimes called 'breath of God'. In the Book of Job, God asks Job, 'Where were you when I laid the foundations of the earth? When the morning stars sang together, and all the sons of God shouted in joy!'

The sacred sound, or word, of creation is *om* (*aum*). The well-known verses from St John's Gospel announce:

'In the Beginning was the Word and the Word was with God, and the Word was God. The same was in the beginning with God. All things were made by him; and without him was not anything made that was made. In him was life; and the light was the light of men. And the light shineth in the darkness; and the darkness comprehended it not.'

It is said that the universe is created from sound and light. The first act of the Creation in several traditions is enshrined in 'God said, 'Let there be light.' The light of Creation was initiated by sound and the speech of God was the origin of the light to which we aspire. It was sound that brought the universe into being. In some Eastern texts, God decided to manifest materiality through divine speech and this is referred to as *saraswati* – the Word. In Chinese Buddhism, the Boddhisattva Kwan Yin is referred to as 'the divine voice.'

There are traces of this word *om* in many languages, such as *shalom* and *salaam*. It may be related to the word *amen* sung after hymns and psalms. It is chanted at the beginning and end of many yoga mantras.

'Om: this eternal word is all; what was, what is and what shall be.'

(Mandukya Upanishad)

Traditionally, chanting *aum* is said to affect the psyche and the entire being. It purifies the body, the emotions, the nervous system and the mind and leads the meditator inwards. It will gradually remove lower negative and selfish desires and habits by destroying the thought patterns that create them. It is a simple regular sound that can be a focus for deep concentration leading to meditation. Through time, regular practice of *aum* will produce in you a gradual change for the better.

How does this sound have such a profound effect on the nervous system? It is energy and sound combined and affects the pituitary gland, which sits at the base of the brain in a position aligned with the space between the eyes. The gland is found in a position at the base of the skull known as *sella turcica*, part of a larger bony portion of the skull, the sphenoid bone. The sphenoid bone is shaped like two wings and the pituitary gland 'rides' on the sphenoid. Directly below the pituitary gland and its bony socket is the hypothalamus of the brain. It controls hunger and thirst and regulates body temperature. The pituitary gland secretes hormones into the bloodstream and plays an important role in body functions. It is the master gland over the other hormones. It regulates growth in all the body cells, the thyroid gland found at the base of the throat, the rate of secretion of the adrenal glands and controls the level of hormones.

When sounding the *aum*, the vibration of the sound causes the sphenoid bone to vibrate, thus setting off a vibration in the *sella turcica* and then in the pituitary gland itself. The vibration therefore plays its part in regulating the function of the gland. So the regular chanting of *aum* plays an important part in our physical and spiritual health. When chanting *aum*, notice how its sound rises over the palate, then to the back of the throat and into the base of the brain.

Recent scientific research has discovered the existence of neuropeptides, intercellular messengers that affect body/mind communication. There is a mind in the body and a body in the mind. The emotions are neuropeptides. Positive thinking and chanting *aum* is a practice that builds neural pathways with beneficial neuropeptides that can enhance our health.[1]

One way of chanting *aum* is to break it up into its component parts. Begin with *aaaaa* and then chant *ooooh – mmmm*. Allow the sound to fade into the distance, into silence. The *aaaaa* that is sounded first is a sound mantra for the heart chakra and takes you into it. *Ooooo* and *mmmm* take you into the crown chakra and as the sound fades into silence you are part of the divine, the universe.

Further evidence about our gifts of co-creation

comes from the Japanese scientist, Masaru Omoto, who photographed water molecules in water that has had prayers said over it. We know also that our body is about seventy per cent water, so chanting *aum* will affect the cells.

Chanting *aum* into an electric transmitter results in the formation of a six-pointed star of colour and light, which is a yoga symbol for the heart chakra.

As a teacher of yoga and meditation, I often lead groups into chanting *aum*. When we chant, I always see angels gathering around the group, like the petals of a beautiful rose of light, enfolding us in angelic radiance.

Several archangels and angels particularly help people to establish the right relationships to all the kingdoms of life – mineral, plants, animal and human, and environmental. All life on planet Earth depends on the environment. The ancient system of the four elements (not to be confused with the periodic table of the elements!) is earth, air, fire and water. There is a fifth element, ether, which is often considered to be the Holy Breath, Holy Spirit or Breath of God.

MUSIC

The Devas and Nature Spirits love music and it attracts them immediately to the place where the music is being played. I love classical music and I frequently go to classical concerts in specialist venues. When I am listening to different pieces I will close my eyes to concentrate better. With my eyes closed I 'see' colours and patterns that the music inspires, which are always different according to the piece of music. At a live concert this is much more likely to happen than when I am listening to recorded music at home. The devotion of the musicians to their music and the instrument they are playing attracts the fairies and nature spirits to the event. There is always a deva that works with the concert hall and holds the energy or blueprint of the intention of the music. It inspires the musicians, the conductor and soloists as well as the enjoyment of the audience. It brings all this devotional energy together so the angels and nature spirits can enhance the atmosphere and charge it up. This is most evident when the audience calls time and again for an encore and calls back the soloists for applause.

Different instruments draw certain nature Spirits. According to the writer Ted Andrews,

• Gnomes and earth spirits like percussion,

drums, rattles, gongs and bells and brass instruments.

- Undines and water spirits like chimes, tubular bells, strings and the voice.
- Sylphs and air spirits like wind instruments, flutes and wind chimes.
- Salamanders and fire sprites like the sistrum, zithers, lyres and harps. (The sistrum is an ancient Egyptian instrument – meaning, literally, that which is being shaken).[1]

ACTIVITY: YOUR FAVOURITE MUSIC

Using the information given above, list three of your favourite pieces of music of different styles and decide which fairies and nature spirits you might attract when playing it. If you play an instrument do it that way, or use a recording.

Well-known composers often seem to hear the music they later write. Sir Edward Elgar, a famous composer of the late nineteenth century and early twentieth century, had an operation in 1918 to remove an infected tonsil, at the time a dangerous operation for a sixty-one-year old. He said he heard music during the operation, and when he regained consciousness, asked for a pencil and paper and wrote down the melody that would

later become the first theme in his cello concerto. It was Jacqueline du Pré who made the concerto world-famous in the 1960s.

At the age of 17, Felix Mendelssohn wrote an overture for the Shakespeare play, 'A Midsummer Night's Dream'. It is said he heard the music and then wrote it down. A contemporary music scholar, George Grove, called it 'the greatest marvel of early maturity that the world has ever seen.' Later, in 1842, Mendelssohn wrote incidental music (Op.61) for a production of the play into which he incorporated the overture. The most famous passage from this is the Wedding March, which surely attracts angels, fairies and nature spirits to the wedding celebrations of numerous couples!

Wolfgang Amadeus Mozart was a prodigious composer from early childhood. There are some claims that listening to his music can improve brain power and recordings have been produced that promote what is called the Mozart effect. There appears to be some controversy over research findings about its benefits but the radio station Classic FM argues that listening to classical music enhances both productivity and brain power. There are also claims that listening to classical music when commuting to work can be just the tonic people need and has been proven to have a positive effect on physical and mental wellbeing. So I think there are nature spirits of music working on uplifting the vibrations and energy of people so that a clearer and healthier atmosphere is available.

Ludwig van Beethoven became profoundly deaf, although he went on writing music he could never hear. It seems as though he heard it inwardly and was then able to write it down.

Not so long ago I attended a classical music concert in the Royal Albert Hall in London. For those who may not know it, this venue is built in a circular manner with a dome. The shape of the concert hall influenced the following vision.

There was a piano recital given by a young pianist in his early twenties making his debut at the venue. The music he was playing was Rachmaninov's Piano Concerto No. 2 in C minor, Opus 18. (This concerto was featured in the David Lean film *Brief Encounter* in 1945.) During the performance of this concerto I had a very spectacular vision of colours, nature spirits and fairies and the deva of music was certainly there. When I am listening to live music, I usually have my eyes closed to enhance the visionary experience. Several years ago I had a similar vision when attending a concert of the same concerto.

I became aware of several colours. The predominant colours were many shades of blue from palest to deep, almost indigo. As the music notes swelled or softened the colours became deeper or paler. There was also a lot of purple and lilac of different shades. Every now and then a clear spring green was visible. Then there began a procession of nature spirits and fairies, who entered into the great dome of the building and proceeded to dance in the manner of old fashioned circle dances or folk dances. There were many of them, all wearing the colours of the musical notes that I saw.

The shape of the building enabled the circular dances to be in harmony with it. As the music began to reach its end the nature sprits and fairies joined hands together and gradually flower petals were formed, creating one great bloom. It grew bigger and bigger until it was like a gigantic lily, but each petal was a different colour. The dome was completely filled with the colours and then its centre began to radiate rays of energy that were like ribbons or streamers of light. The ribbons of light reached out to each member of the audience (nearly five thousand people!), according to the colour needed by the person.

The players were given a standing ovation and many cheers and altogether it was a most uplifting experience. There is certainly a specific kind of energy at a live performance as I don't see anything like this when listening to a cd or watching a TV recording. The energy of the audience and the musicians combine together to provide the energy for the nature spirits to respond to it and create the vision and rays of light and colour.

The twentieth-century spiritual teacher White Eagle has this to say about the angels of music.

'There is nothing like harmonious music for creating harmony in a soul. In the new age, sound and music play a very big part. Sound and music provoke feeling: through feeling and imagination you develop gifts of the spirit, yet feeling and

ACTIVITY:
A L'APRES MIDI D'UN FAUNE

One of the composers who wrote about nature spirits was Claude Debussy, whose prelude 'A l'Après-Midi d'un Faune' (The Afternoon of a Faun) has become famous. The music depicts a faun alone in the woods, where he is playing his panpipes. He is disturbed by passing nymphs and naiads and chases them until he is tired and falls into a sleep filled with dreams.

The music is played by flutes, oboes, cor anglais, clarinets, bassoons, horns, harps and strings.

The instruments which are used by Debussy are the clue to the type of nature spirits that the music attracts. Can you make a brief note of what they are?

Edouard Manet's illustration for 'A L'Apré-Midi d'un Faune' (Public Domain)

imagination are the very qualities which many people need help to develop. This is why beautiful music is necessary. It can contribute to the awakening and development of a man or woman's feeling.'[1]

Here are some further thoughts from White Eagle, from the book SPIRITUAL UNFOLDMENT I:

'Music is a tremendous power and it can be said that it is at the very heart of creation. Some people can walk in their garden and every flower that blooms would be a note of music to them. To some people the love felt for friends and family is music too. The exquisite love which they have experienced is a great symphony. Music is not just the sounds from a musical instrument but the divine sound of creation.'[2]

CELEBRATIONS

The spiritual group were having their annual Christmas Fair. The atmosphere was full of excitement as people met their friends again. There was an excited hubbub of chatter as people exchanged their latest news and looked at all the beautiful artefacts that were on offer. There were vegetarian and vegan foods to buy, healthy and delicious teas, sandwiches and cakes to eat. The scent of essential oils and flowers wafted from the stalls and there was a good selection of quality crystals to choose.

It was not just the people who were excited! The atmosphere was absolutely electric with the enthusiasm of the fairies and nature spirits who gathered there. The unseen world was busy with its preparations before the people had started theirs. The deva of the centre had already sent out a clarion call to the fairy world. The deva was holding the thoughts and ideas of everyone together so that the spiritual centre would fulfil its purpose by being available to people to come and share this occasion. The fairies enjoyed being with people who believed in them, could see them and hear them.

There were gnomes who worked with crystals deep in the earth and the plants that sent their roots into the soil. Sylphs wafted the aromas of the plants, essential oils and flowers around the hall. Salamanders inspired customers to buy scented candles and incenses to bring (safe) living flames into their homes with both fire and scents. There were undines present with the essential oil blends –an alchemical process whereby 'in distillation of the oils the spirit of the plant is released and preserved. The more you honour the spirit of the oil, the more it will teach you'.[1]

All the colour, aromas and vibration combined to make it possible for people to share at a deeper level the love, light and devotion with the fairies and nature spirits, as well as the presiding deva.

We shall see later how certain seasons of the year attract a special blessing and that each season has its particular devic and angelic energy which works with nature spirits.

TO CONNECT WITH A PLANT'S ENERGY

Tune in to a plant's energy. Breathe slowly and gently. You may see the shining form of the plant deva, all light and colour. It will be working with you to use the plant in its intended way. Shower the plant with love from your heart chakra, assuring it you will use it only for its highest good. Trust what it tells you. Notice any pictures, symbols, images, feelings or ideas that come to you.

THE NATURAL WORLD

Summer is the time when our gardens and parks are filled with the colour and scent of flowers. In my garden I have irises, roses, hardy geraniums and campanula. There are several bushes of lavender. The bees love the cotoneaster bush, which is filled with them in spring when it flowers. Elementals and Angels love to draw our attention to the beauty of nature and we can learn to be aware of them through the colour and perfume of flowers. Angels bring healing qualities to flowers and essential oils and flower remedies will help you to make the contact if you don't have the flowers available.

The natural world around us all is filled with colour and magic and healing. One of the best ways to become rejuvenated is to go for a walk in a beautiful place nearby (I'll write of my local park shortly). One of the most magical places I have visited was the Keukenhof Gardens in Holland one spring. It is described as one of the most beautiful places in the world and one of the ten places everyone should visit. More than seven million tulips, daffodils and hyacinths are planted every year in thirty-two hectares of the garden and fill the air with their fragrance.

When I went, the winter had been cold and I had a painful back. We booked a long weekend in

April. The sun came out and the sight of acres of many coloured spring flowers was wonderful. I felt very much better at the end of the visit and am convinced that the colours and perfumes of the natural world and its flowers had magical healing benefits for me. They reminded me of the rainbow bridge, the bridge to the world of light, for all the colours of the spectrum are found in flowers. When we breathe in the beautiful scent of flowers brought to us by the breeze, we are renewed in spirit.

A few years ago I was doing some spiritual training with a Native American teacher in Texas. My teacher told me to forget what I had learned about the way the ancient indigenous people had learnt about the healing and spiritual properties of plants.

'Did you think,' she asked, 'that in those days, the medicine people ate a tiny portion of the plant and waited to see what would happen? No, that wasn't how they found out. They sat with the plant and tuned in to it. The plant told them how to use it. We can still do it, if we learn how to practise and if we radiate love and respect to it.'

She got me to sit with trees and plants and ask them to tell me how they should be used. As I was on a different continent I did not always know what the tree or plant was so I could not have any preconceived ideas about them. She didn't tell me what they were until afterwards. It's a good idea to give the plant a gift before you tune in to it, she told me. A hair from your head is a good one. The first two entries of my diary, below, were from trees I recognized but I was given information I didn't know. Great trees have their own nature spirits.

Diary Entry 1 – The Fig Tree Deva

I sat under a fig tree in the warm sun. I asked it what it could do for me and what its healing is. I realized it gladly gave of its shade from the hot sun. It was cooling, and its fruit was cooling and cleansing for the body. It told me its leaves could be used for a poultice or dressing on the skin to draw out inflammation.

Then a beautiful female tree deva stood before me. Her colours were dark green and purple, the colour of the tree and its fruit. She welcomed me and gave me her blessing because she knew I would not misuse the gifts of the tree – by chopping it down for firewood or the like.

Diary Entry 2 - The Deva of the Banana Tree

I sat in the shade of a banana tree. My teacher was cross with me because I told her I don't like bananas! This is because there were none available in the UK when I was a child during World War 2 and I was 10 before I really had one. She made me apologize to the tree as I had hurt its feelings!

I felt deliciously cool and strengthened in the shade of the tree because its large shady leaves filled me with courage. I gave the tree some dried herbs I had brought from my garden at home – roses, jasmine and lavender – and hairs from my head. This gave the tree greetings from the guardian of my own land (the garden) in London and the other spirits there. The hairs gave the love of my personal energy (my DNA) and in return the tree gave me its own energy, the gift of shade.

It told me it was glad I didn't misuse its energy by buying its fruit from those who exploit the land and its trees – governments and multinational corporations and dishonest growers. I try to buy from ethical companies and fairtrade schemes as much as I can. Because I had given love and blessings to the tree, it told me that this would apply to all the banana trees everywhere. Any bananas I ate from that time would strengthen me, especially when I am hot and hungry.

The large leaves would be glad to be used by me for weaving and thatching. It told me that in future I would grow to love to eat bananas. They can be eaten fresh or dried or baked in their skin.

A male tree deva stood before me. He was dressed in green and yellow and I asked forgiveness for saying I didn't like bananas. He graciously granted it!

Diary Entry 3 – An Oak Tree

I did not know what kind of tree this one was as it didn't look like a British oak, but later I discovered it was a local variety of oak. It was very tall and straight, very stately. I gave the tree some of the herbs and flowers from my garden at home and I wrapped some of my hairs around its twigs. I leaned against its trunk, resting the front of my body and forehead on it and my arms were around its trunk. I felt very at home with it.

I could really relax with this tree and release my personal boundaries and stress. I felt as if I could actually melt into the tree. Its quality was strength through being able to relax and let go of what we hold onto through rigidity and fear. It was strength through letting go, dissolving and relaxing.

The spirit of the tree was a wise old man dressed in a grey-green robe. The colour grey represented the friendship of the tree spirit and green was for strength through adaptability and dependability. He gave me a staff from an oak branch. I discovered it was a variety of oak quite unknown to me.

There is a Bach Flower remedy made from oak. It is the remedy for the person who fights life through all its difficulties and never gives up. Its key word is perseverance.

Diary Entry 4 – Another Oak

The next tree was another species unknown to me, but I discovered it to be yet another variety of oak. I shared my herbs and hair with the tree. It had dropped two of its leaves onto the chair where I was to sit. I held a leaf between my two palms. Suddenly I felt weak and shaky.

The tree said, 'See how tall and straight I am. When you feel weak and shaky and your body trembles, take scrapings from my bark. Boil them and drink the tea for strength.' I connected with the spirit of the leaf. Like all children, it liked to leap and run. Drinking the tea or taking the Bach oak essence would make me feel strong and youthful.

We are part of a living world. It is important to reconnect with that natural world and learn to live in harmony with it, to honour all life as the indigenous people of former generations, like Chief Seattle (see opposite), knew how to. It is time we learned to respect the earth planet and her gifts and to restore that ancient partnership.

THE CEDAR TREE

Near where I live there is a park with a beautiful cedar tree. I love to lean on its tree trunk and feel its strength and energy seeping into me. It provides shade and is so tall it's difficult to photograph. When it is really hot and sunny the needles and branches make amazing patterns as the sun shines through them and the branches. There are wonderful patterns and shadows and the tree is very wise.

The needles fill the air with their fragrance and it gives a gift of cones which can be used in floral or Christmas decorations. If you live in an area where you can have a fire they release their fragrance when burning. Cedarwood essential oil is

Every part of the earth is sacred, every shining pine needle, every sandy shore, every light mist in the dark forest, every clearing, and every winged creature is sacred to my people.

We are part of the earth and it is part of us.

The fragrant flowers are our sisters, the deer and mighty eagle are our brothers; the rocky peak, the fertile meadows, all things are connected like the blood that unites a family.

Chief Seattle

know the secrets of the devic kingdom love to sit under it or commune with it by leaning against its trunk. From a distance, if you open your inner vision, you can see its enormous aura sending out love, strength and healing to the whole area.'

DR EDWARD BACH

Using his own subtle awareness, in the twentieth century Dr Edward Bach discovered the healing system now known as Bach Flower Remedies. The system is best described as a homeopathic or vibrational one. Bach became dissatisfied with his previously successful medical practice and began to rely on his natural gifts of intuition and as a healer. He began to work with the flowers, herbs and trees that grew around him in the English countryside and discovered the remedies that healed a particular mental or emotional state. He believed that these states were the underlying cause of disease when he experienced negative feelings, and he would hold his hands over different plants and flowers until he found one that healed the emotional or mental state he was experiencing. The remedies are made by soaking flowers in spring water in the early morning sun.

strengthening and fortifying. It gives the will to be firm in challenging situations. The age of the tree is unknown but the manor house nearby is nearly four hundred years old – it was built in 1622,.

Its wisdom has stored in its memory all the local events over the centuries and the deva that cares for it is very proud of its age and strength.

The deva told me, 'This venerable tree has sheltered and supported many over its years. Children have played in its shade, dogs have happily flopped down to rest there after their games and squirrels play in its branches. Many birds have nested and settled there over the years and insects and spiders hide in the rugged trunk with its many hiding places. People like yourself who

You can investigate this for yourself when you are out in the country. At dawn when the sun has

ATTUNEMENT TO ANGELS OF THE NATURAL WORLD

Put one or two drops of angelica oil in a vaporizer to scent the air. Centre yourself with gentle breathing. Feel each breath in the nostrils as you breathe in and out. Follow the breath as it enters your chest. Feel your breath breathing you. Begin to visualize a shining sun above your head. As you breathe in, visualize yourself being filled with light, which floods your whole being. Feel as if every atom and cell is radiating light like millions of tiny suns. Feel yourself rising upwards, as if on wings of light, along a path of light, into the world of light. See this path, as a shaft of light shining in front of you, as you travel up it.

Find yourself in a beautiful garden. It is summer and the sun is shining as you walk with bare feet across the grass. The grass feels soft and velvety under your feet. There are beds of flowers of many colours on each side of the path and the warm air is filled with a beautiful scent. You feel filled with peace and tranquillity. In front of you is a magnificent rose arbour. Bushes of white roses climb up and around it. The arbour is built in the shape of a large circle with white trellissed panels. At each side of the circle is an arched entrance, forming a temple of white roses. Inside the circle are white marble benches. At the centre is a beautiful fountain, which rises from a white marble basin in the shape of a rose. The water rises up into the air and rainbow mists form in the spray as the sun catches the water droplets.

Tune in to the devas and nature spirits. Devas of fire and warmth are in the sunlight. Water devas bring refreshment from the fountain. Nature spirits and flower fairies create the gentle sweet scent of the roses.

Sit on one of the benches. Decide on an issue you may wish to ask about.

Visualize an angel coming to sit beside you and ask for its name. Tune in to experience what it looks like.

Do you visualize colours?

Light?

How do you feel?

What changes in your body tell you that you are in the presence of an angel or deva?

Do you feel

- hot or cold?
- a tingling sensation?

- goosebumps?

Does your hair feel as if it's standing on end?

There is no need to feel fearful as these are clear indications you are in the presence of a spiritual being.

Don't dismiss anything as only imagination. Ask questions or discuss any problems that concern you at this time. Listen to the messages you hear mentally. Have a mental conversation with the deva or angel and listen to her replies. With practice you will know which thoughts are yours and which are the replies of the deva.

Know that angels of light surround you and the planet earth. Spiritual strength and inspiration is flowing into us and the planet from the spiritual realms that surround us so that people can make progress in spiritual understanding. Ask, and you will be given all the inspiration you need to help you. This may come in the meditation itself or in some other way at another time.

When you are ready, conclude your meditation in the usual way.

just risen is the best time. Hold your left hand (the receiving hand) over flowers and, following the instructions on p. 39, feel the vibration or any other sensation you experience, that comes from it. You might also become aware of the elemental being that cares for the plant.

There is more on Dr Bach and his remedies on p. 84.

ANGELICA

There is a very special plant that helps us to connect with angels. It is Angelica root (*Angelica Archangelica*). It has special abilities to help us with confidence, clarity, spiritual inspiration and connection to angels. With it, you may like to use the affirmation, 'I am surrounded by the loving energy of angels and archangels and their inspiration is always available to me'.

This plant is well known because the stems are crystallized in sugar and used in cake decoration. It is sometimes called angel's grass. The plant is called after the archangels 'because of its angelical virtues. It is an herb of the sun.' (Culpeper) As a herb of the sun, it is associated with Archangel Michael and, like his sword, it can help to cut through illusions, helping us to face our shadow self and to develop more spiritually as we become self-aware. It assists in helping us to connect with our spiritual nature.

Angelica is an expensive oil. I burn this oil when connecting with angels and at workshops when needing to attune to higher spiritual vibrations. Invite Archangel Michael and all Angels of Light to join you when using it for meditation or if facilitating a workshop. For personal use, it will also help you to connect with your own guardian angel, which is with you from birth. Use the words in the next section to attune to your guardian angel or when you need to contact angels and devas of nature for particular advice.

SOME FINAL WORDS

I'd like to close this section with some very special words from White Eagle, and a picture I took in the house which spoke of an angel presence to me.

'We want you to understand that an angel is not a human being, but is a great force, a power. And because it is a great power, it is concentrated in a form which man, when his eyes are open, can understand. So the form is that of a very illumined being, like a man, with a human face, for instance.

These angelic forces are emitting great streams of light from the head and shoulders. They are like rays of light. So, if you see angelic beings you will know that what appear to be wings are forces and streams of light.

'Climb the mountains and you can sense a great power – you are then responding to the deva of the mountain. Then again, how fascinating do you find water, flowing in a great river, tumbling in waterfalls. It is the same – you are responding to the deva. It is the same with the sun, the power of fire; and with the air. And so, my children, thank God for the elements and for the power, the food, the sustenance which all receive. It is the etheric power which brings to fruition the physical grain and the fruits of the earth. And all this etheric life is controlled and directed by the Great Spirit. If you would have health and all you need – not necessarily all you want – but all you need for the harmonious and beautiful and joyous life, learn to meditate upon these God-given forces.'

White Eagle

SECTION TWO
Angels and Devas of the Elements

Chapter Two

THE ANGELS, DEVAS AND NATURE SPIRITS OF THE EARTH

THE ELEMENT EARTH supports us. It is our material world, where we live and earn our living, caring for our physical bodies, and also caring for the Earth, Mother Earth, herself. The devas and angels of Earth help with our work, our resources, money and possessions, home and security, education and society and the environment. Earth represents *strength* and this element helps us with our connection to planet Earth and to all of nature and the material world.

Its colour is green and in springtime all the plants really begin to flower and the trees burst into leaves and blossoms. The Earth looks as though it is covered by beautiful green mist as the leaves on the trees begin to grow. Bees and butterflies are seen and birds sing loudly. Devas and angels of Earth help us to understand our oneness with all creatures – animals, insects, birds, fish, plants, crystals, rocks and minerals and how the whole of life is interconnected. As an example of this, in 2012 there was news of wild elephants in Africa that went to mourn the passing of an 'elephant whisperer', a man who cared for elephants. Two herds of elephants walked in procession from different parts of Africa to mourn him at the house where he died. It's a miraculous example of the oneness of all life.[1]

Gnomes are the elementals of the Earth. They work with the rocks and minerals of the earth and have great strength and power over the natural world. They work with gemstones, precious stones and metals. They live in underground caves and are said to be guardians of hidden treasure. If you have a gnome in your garden, he will usually prefer to be in a dark area, under bushes or the shadiest part. They like to live in and under tree roots. A friend of mine sees fairies and gnomes very clearly and told me I had a gnome living in the garden. After tuning in, he gave me his name, Trusty. I have tuned in to gnomes and other elementals that live along London railway embankments. Embankments are a rich source of wild life, herbs and plants. In the human body, gnomes and earth elementals work with the bones, which are its densest parts.

Gnomes serve the Earth.

The spiritual message of the Earth element is service, and the devas and angels of the Earth help us to realize the interconnectedness of all life. The Earth is not dark, but is full of fire and light. When we look at photos of the planet taken from space, it is like a beautiful jewel of light shining in the darkness of space. The angels, devas and elementals of Earth inspire us with longing to care for all human life and of nature. They are the inspiration behind those who seek to safeguard our environment.

Attune to these devas and angels for health, security, resources, education and the community and the environment. They will help you if you are planning home improvements, or a beautiful garden. They will assist you to care for your physical body in a loving way, for instance by having an essential oil massage; or a pleasant walk in the countryside; digging or tending your garden; climbing a mountain or by following a healthy organic diet. If you would like a more beautiful home these are the angels who will help you to make the best of what you can afford. Visualize the beauty that you long for and ask the angels to help you create it. Play soothing music and burn essential oils or incense to bring the nature kingdom closer. Keep crystals and gemstones, beautiful ornaments and flowers and plants in your rooms. As you create beauty and order in your life, you will spread it all around you. Yoga as a system of bodywork is popular with people who have the sun in Earth signs, which are Capricorn, Taurus and Virgo.

The Earth element brings a great feeling of peace, safety and stability. The keywords for the help of Earth angels and nature spirits are *stability, nurturing, loving, caring, building, maintaining* and *sustaining*. They remind us of the Native American chant about the earth being our mother.

'Mother I feel you under my feet,

'Mother, I feel your heartbeat.'

MEDITATION WITH GAIA, THE EARTH MOTHER

Sit outside in a place where you feel safe and at home or in a comfortable chair, making sure your back is straight and your breathing is free. Feel your feet are firmly connected to the ground. Remove your shoes so this connection can be clearly felt. You may feel warmth or tingling in the souls of your feet.

As you breathe deeply, create a ribbon of light from your heart chakra and chest down through your spine to the base (*muladhara*) chakra. Continue to breathe the ribbon of pure light down through into the ground at your feet. There is a chakra under your feet called the earth star chakra. Breathe gently and deeply in and out of the earth star chakra.

Visualize it as a gleaming star. Perhaps it is black like tourmaline or gold like amber. Or you may see it quite differently. Continue to feel the sensations in the soles of your feet and your connection to Earth.

Now begin to breathe the ribbon of light down into the ground and see it travelling through the soil, roots, minerals and gemstones, and then the rocks of the Earth. Finally it reaches into the centre of the planet. There you become one with Gaia and her beating heart. See it as fire and light – but it doesn't burn. Breathe in and out in time with the beating of Gaia's heart. Spend some time in silence with your breath and Gaia's breath. Gaia is the planetary angel. She may have a message or a gift for you.

When you feel ready, thank Gaia for her gift of life and strength and breathe your way back up the ribbon of light. Once again see it travelling through the rocks, the gemstones and minerals, the roots and soil to the earth star chakra. Feel any sensations in your feet that tell you of the connection you have made with Gaia, the planetary angel. Continue to breathe back up the spine with the ribbon of light until you reach your heart chakra again. Breathe a few times and then open your eyes.

ACTIVITY: A MEDITATION WALK

It is good to walk barefoot on the earth and feel its beauty and power. Attune to Mother Earth and feel her life force and energy entering your feet and rising up through the body. With each footstep repeat, aloud or mentally, 'thank you, thank you, and thank you.' Thank the earth for all her gifts.

As you take your meditation walk, stop every six steps and observe what is around you. Notice birdsong and birds, insects, the sound of the wind rustling the leaves or grass, patterns in the clouds. If you have a mobile phone or camera with you, take a snapshot to put in your journal.

You can also collect things that will remind you of your walk. You might notice pebbles, flowers or leaves to press, feathers, small branches or twigs that have blown down in the wind. If you are walking on a beach, there will be shells and pebbles, perhaps driftwood. You can make a collection of these and find a small stick or branch, tie a selection of things to it to make a bundle or keep a collection to use as a meditation memory later.

ARCHANGEL ARIEL

Archangel Ariel is an angel of the earth element. She is often seen with a lion by her side, symbol of courage and strength. Her name means 'Lion of God'. Her message to us is

'I give you the strength and stability you need to be grounded firmly on the Earth.

I give you your foundations

And help you with all your relationships

Whether they are human, animal, plants, trees, or crystals,

Devas or nature spirits.

I send you friends, pets and the support you need

And guide you to the right work experiences.

I provide all you need to nurture you,

The flowers that bloom with bright colours

And fill the air with sweet perfumes

Created by the fairies that care for them..

I send you the fruits, vegetables and grains that nourish your body.

Remember I am always with you

Surrounding you with love and guidance

And wisdom from the Earth.'

MEDITATION FOR ARIEL AND THE ANGELS AND NATURE SPIRITS OF EARTH: WAKE UP TO LIFE!

As you wake up, breathe health and energy into your body. Feel yourself becoming one with the earth, who is like a mother in providing all our needs. She provides all the food we need, which grows in the rich soil of the planet Earth, Gaia.

Affirm: *'Thank you for this new day.'*
'The Earthly Mother, her angels and I are one.
'All the health and strength I need come from her.
'She cares for me and I do my best to care for her.'

Breathe deeply and feel your lungs filling with life-giving energy. Surround yourself with light. Breathe it in and breathe it down into your body and out through your legs and feet into the ground, the Earthly Mother. Visualize a cord or ribbon of light extending down into the earth, through the soil, the stones and gemstones, roots and minerals until it is deep into the core of Mother Earth. It is like an anchor that keeps you safely grounded.

Breathing in, draw the energy up again, through the earth and into your spine. See it moving up through your spine until it reaches the crown chakra. Continue to breathe your ribbon of light up until it reaches the sun. You are safely anchored between earth and heaven. Breathe the light of the sun into your heart chakra. You are surrounded and filled with pure golden light.

As you look into the light, you see the beautiful form of the archangel Ariel. and her nature spirit helpers. She looks like a goddess of nature, with long flowing hair, or like your ideal picture of woman. She is dressed in robes of green, with the colours of flowers, herbs and grasses, cereals and food plants adorning her. On her head is a crown of flowers. A beautiful golden lion sits beside her. The Earth is hers and she will heal it from the pollution and exploitation it has been subjected to, but she tells you she needs your help to do it.

Every person who can live in a sustainable way to the best of their ability helps to heal the planet. She asks you what you can do to help, so tell her. Feel surrounded by the protective cloak of Ariel. She radiates even more light to you, which strengthens and sustains your ideas. You begin to feel the rhythm of the earth, of her heartbeat. Begin to feel at one with everything around you and see the beauty of nature, of trees and plants, insects and the blue sky. Thank them for their blessing. Then they leave and you feel encouraged and strengthened by them

Conclude your meditation in the usual way.

All flowers have their own deva as well as flower fairies. The best place to meet them is somewhere like a secret garden. Most people will be familiar with the story or film, *The Secret Garden*, based on the story by Frances Hodgson Burnett, and the magical place it was. You can create your own secret garden, a place in your imagination. Imagination is the gateway to clairvoyance, so don't let people tell you something is just imagination. The secret garden of your mind is a safe place to visit for rest and rejuvenation.

LAVENDER

One of our best-loved English flowers is lavender. There are many varieties and it can grow in dry and stony conditions. The angels tell me that one of the ways that we can help to heal Planet Earth is to make sacred circles and place crystals in the circle. I have several lavender bushes which have self-seeded into a medicine wheel I made. It is formed of white stones from a Welsh beach set in gravel. The lavender thrives there although there is almost no soil to it, being on a plastic base laid under the gravel.

The white stones contain tiny quartz crystals, which can be seen in the holes left in them by the pounding of the waves. There are also large quartz crystals and rose quartz pieces in the circle. The circle can be made with herbs and flowers in any suitable part of the garden, or on a windowsill or plant pot if you live in a flat without your own garden. This can then be a focus for your angel meditations and earth healing. The devas of the earth, of the plants and crystals, tell us that making sacred circles is one of the ways we can help to heal the environment. This can be a focus for earth healing and meditations.

Lavender provides essential oils for soap and perfume and lavender bags to hang in the wardrobes and put in the drawers. This helps to keep away moths and scents clothes and bed linen. The angel message of lavender is healing through cleanliness. It is also a powerful antiseptic and can assist in the healing of cuts, burns and insect bites. It lowers blood pressure and helps in sleeplessness. Put two or three drops on a tissue and keep it under the pillow when you find sleep elusive. Do not use it neat if you have sensitive skin.

The deva of lavender appears in many different shades from pale to deepest lavender. You can tune into her when you use the essential oil or plants or the perfume. Ask her to keep you and your house refreshed and healthy. Think of her when you are using it. Notice the pictures and ideas that you have as that is how angels inspire you. Remember to get the right lavender product, as some of the perfumes used are artificial and don't carry the healing energy. The name to look for is *lavandula officinalis*.

ROSES

June is the month when all the roses are out in England. Roses are the flowers of love. Stella Rose is the name of the angel of roses but she is more than that. She radiates the divine feminine and is the angel of the Rose Star. This is an ancient mystical order of angels and master souls who work with and through humanity as they seek to become one with divine love. They are masters of the heart and its balanced energy. They work to heal the human heart from the hurts and stresses of earthly life and the tests, which come to everybody. An angel or guide of this order will stand by silently radiating the healing rays of the rose star. Stella Rose works with healers.

The sweetest perfume is found in old-fashioned roses. If you want to use rose essential oil, the best kind is rose otto, and although it is expensive it is the purest. *Rosa Damascena, Rosa centifolia* and *Rosa gallica* are all varieties used.

Nicholas Culpeper, the seventeenth-century herbalist, considered the rose to be uplifting to the mind in depression. It is also helpful for insomnia, as it quietens the mind. In traditional aromatherapy, rose is used as a heart tonic and used for insomnia as well as grief. Rose calms and supports the heart and restores a sense of wellbeing. The damask rose is the holy rose, considered to be a symbol of God's love to the world. When Bernadette had her vision of Mary at Lourdes, roses surrounded her. Mother Mary is also known as the Queen of the Angels.

As well as being associated with the physical heart, the rose is taken as a symbol of the heart chakra, the energy centre associated with the physical heart and the thymus gland.

In meditation on a rose, the centre of the rose displays a diamond-like drop of dew. As it radiates light, it takes on the appearance of a brilliant star. The heart chakra is the place where the reflection of the divine is found. The yogis refer to this as *atman*, that spark of the divine hidden in everyone. It is said that God hid him/herself in the only place people would never think to look: that is, within their own heart.

STELLA ROSE

*I am Stella Rose
The angel of the rose star.
Inhale the scent of roses
And open your heart chakra.
Visualize my beautiful shades of roses,
Roses of all colours
That fill your heart, the jewel of divine love,
With happiness and harmony
Sit in the centre of the rose,
Cradled within its petals
Of love and protection.
As you inhale the scent of roses, the flower of divine unconditional love
Experience its vibration filling your whole being
Until every atom and cell
Is filled with it.*

A MEDITATION ON THE ROSE

Affirmation: *'May the jewel in the rose of my heart burn brightly, bringing about spiritual illumination.'*

Sit for meditation using a rose from your garden, rose oil or a picture of a rose.

Visualize a brilliant light like the sun or a radiant star shining above you. Breathe in its light and feel it shining like a laser down through your crown centre (chakra), down through your spine into your chest and heart chakra.

Continue to breathe in this light and see it shining on to a beautiful rosebud in the centre of your chest, the heart chakra. Observe the rose and its colour.

As the light continues to shine onto the rose, see the petals begin to open. The petals open wide. Deep in the heart of the rose, which is also your heart, you see a small drop of dew. The light pours down onto the drop of dew and it becomes brilliant like a diamond.

The rose becomes a full-blown rose with a brilliant diamond, the jewel of enlightenment, deep in its heart. This diamond, the jewel of enlightenment, is always there, waiting for you to discover it. Then you truly know yourself.

When you are ready to close your meditation, visualize the petals of the rose closing again to protect the jewel.

DAISIES

I have always been fascinated by daisies, and I remember painting them years ago. I wonder if children still like to make daisy chains as I used to. A garland of daisies can be worn like a crown. Garlands represent good luck and the connection between this world and the next. The circle represents the love of God, which always surrounds us.

The daisy gets its name from the old name for it, the day's eye, because the flower opens in the morning and closes in the evening. It is associated with purity and innocence and also as an indication of love. Petals would be pulled off a flower one by one, with the saying, 'He loves me, he loves me not.' The last petal indicated the strength of love between sweethearts. In herbalism, the crushed fresh leaves are used to treat bruises and swellings and an old name for a daisy is bruisewort.

A MEDITATION ON DAISIES

Sit quietly in your meditation place. Play relaxing music and burn incense or essential oils. Breathe in slowly and deeply. Notice how your breath flows into your lungs and causes your tummy to move outwards. Breathe out by just relaxing your chest and abdomen. Repeat a few breaths and notice when you become relaxed and serene. Your breath is breathing you.

Then in front of you, see a path. Follow the path through a beautiful lawn until you come to an old brick wall, which is a rosy golden colour as the sun shines on it. There is a gate in the wall. Visualize the gate. What colour is it? What is the handle like? Is it locked? – and if so, where is the key hidden? Perhaps you see a friendly bird sitting on top of the wall singing to you. In the story *The Secret Garden* it was a robin.

When you are ready, turn the handle and open the gate and walk into the garden. This is your secret garden, your secret spiritual retreat that you can go to whenever you like. You can meet your spirit guide or guardian angel, or the deva of all daisies, or any of the archangels there.

Look around and see what it is like. Create everything as you would like it to be in your 'imagination'. Decide what the flowerbeds will have in them, the colours of the flowers; imagine benches to sit, maybe a fountain or pool. Walk through your garden admiring its beauty.

You come to a wilder place, like a wildflower meadow. The grass is soft and warm in the sunshine so you sit down on it. You are surrounded by daisies and you enjoy the sight of their purity and whiteness. You look up and see the daisy deva as a beautiful angelic being in shades of white and silver with a big golden heart centre, just like the daisy itself. There are indications of pink around her, like the daisies have. She reminds us of the children's song (with words by Jan Struther),

> 'Daisies are our silver,
> Buttercups our gold:
> This is all the treasure
> We can have and hold.'

We don't need to be surrounded by material possessions, because simplicity and friendship are the most important things in life. The daisy loves the sun and is at its best in the sunshine, in the same way that we too feel better and more cheerful in the sun. Daisies show themselves in the first sunny warmth of spring and are one of the first signs of the weather getting warmer. Visualize the angel coming close to you until you are surrounded by her aura. You feel filled with sweetness and light and as her colours wash over you it is like being in a shower of silvery, white light shot through with golden warmth. Her wings enfold you and you feel a sense of deep peace. She may have a special message for you if you listen carefully.

When it is time to leave the angel, she gives you a bunch of daisies as a reminder of her. It reminds you that the best spiritual development is simplicity. You walk back through the garden until you reach the door and open it. Walk out of the garden and back along the path. The friendly bird sings to you as you leave the garden. Once again, become aware of your breath, and when you are ready open your eyes.

THE GREEN MAN

The Green Man is well known in the British tradition. You can see images of him on old buildings, particularly on old cathedrals. He is seen as a 'mask' of foliage, hiding amongst the leaves in forests and hedges. He is known in different forms internationally – on churches and cathedrals throughout Europe and temples in India. It is thought that he was created in churches by stonemasons who were secretly pagan at a time when the church forbade their beliefs.

He represents the power of nature that eventually wins against the changes made by humans. Weeds and wild flowers spring up through cracks in pavements and drives and even push their way through concrete. Ancient temples and pyramids have been discovered that for hundreds of years have been buried and hidden in forests and mountains. The Green Man is also included in Morris Dances and as the Green King in Mummers Plays. He represents the power of nature and the flow of the seasons and of all life from birth to transition.

My pottery Green Man always seems to hide himself away in the garden!

BRING THE GREEN MAN INTO YOUR LIFE

I have a Green Man plaque that hangs on my garden fence. He stands for an ancient tradition I've set out after this exercise. I can hardly ever find my Green Man in the summer as he is so hidden by the luxuriant growth of the passion flower hedge that surrounds him. When the foliage drops in winter, he is clearly seen.

Walking out of doors in nature is important for our health and well-being. Even in the city there are parks where you can go to become aware of the natural life of the trees and flowers. It also helps to keep you grounded in a world where we seem to live more and more in our heads because of all the technology we rely on. Recently I was walking in my local park when I noticed what looked like a face in the leaves of a distant tree. It was the way the pattern of the leaves grew but it was definitely the Green Man that I could see.

If you are going through a challenging time and need answers, try this helpful visualization.

Centre yourself by tuning in to your breathing and feel yourself growing peaceful and calm. If music helps you, find some forest sounds to create the ambience of walking in woodland, listening to the birdsong and the rustle of the wind in the trees. You might be able to record birdsong and breezes on a smartphone. (In spite of my remark about modern technology, it does have its uses!)

Visualize the sun shining above your head. As you breathe, rays of light begin to surround you until you feel that you are sitting in a canopy of sunlight. Warm rays of light fill your whole being as you breathe, and you feel yourself rising and travelling upwards on a path of light until you find yourself in a beautiful forest glade. Mighty trees surround you. There are fir trees as well as other woodland trees like oak, beech, sycamore, rowan and elder.

The glade is a clearing like a great circle filled with soft green grass. Wild flowers of many colours bloom in it. On each side of the circle you see a path leading into the centre of the clearing. You are standing on one of the paths and there is one at the centre of the circle on your right, one to the left and another ahead of you on the opposite side of the circle. It is like a natural medicine wheel or sacred circle with a path at each of the four directions – east, south, west and north.

Walk into the circle, feeling the softness of the grass beneath your feet. Smell the delicate scent of the wildflowers. The sun is warm and refreshing breezes bring fragrant scents of trees, shrubs and flowers. There are brightly coloured butterflies and you can hear the songs of woodland birds and the hum of insects.

When you reach the centre of the clearing, there is a beautiful spring of clear water that bubbles up between rocks and stones in the ground. It spreads out to form a shallow pool with a clear sandy floor. You stoop down, cupping your hands to drink the cool, refreshing water. It tastes so fresh and sweet it is like the elixir of life. As you splash your face and head and bathe your feet you begin to feel totally alive and invigorated. Looking at the sandy floor of the pool, you see something shining in it. It is a beautiful coloured pebble, worn smooth by the water that constantly bubbles into the pool from the spring. You bend down to pick it up, examining its colour, texture and markings.

It is a green gemstone that has been waiting for you to come and find it. Its surface has been polished by the ages of the time that it has spent lying in the bubbling spring waiting for you. Its special gift for you is to bring more inspiration and creativity into your life and work.

Sit by the pool enjoying the warmth of the sun. Then you feel that someone is coming towards you. You recognize him as he is dressed in all the shades of forest green, of plants and grasses. He is carrying a staff. You notice him standing in front of you. He is wearing a green robe and has a wreath of leaves in his hair. It is the Green Man.

You are pleased to see him. Tell him about any challenges you are facing at this time and ask for advice. Remember what comes into your mind. It might be pictures, symbols or colours, which all have meaning to your situation. He sits beside you and you are able to ask his advice about improving your work life, applying for promotion, changing jobs or finding more congenial work. Discuss any issues you wish with him. You may hear advice, see symbols, or get ideas. All of these things help you to heal your life and to be joyful and fulfilled. Be ready to consider any likely possibilities.

Thank the Green Man and turn to go back across the clearing and along the path, travelling down the pathway of light back into your everyday self. Begin to breathe more deeply and open your eyes when you are ready. Take some time to feel sure that you are grounded once again into everyday consciousness, and take some deep breaths and walk on when you are ready..

Chapter Three

THE ANGELS, DEVAS AND NATURE SPIRITS OF THE AIR

THE FIRST THING we do when we are born is to take a deep lungful of fresh air. Then we release it with our first cry! The first element of earth that we bond with is air, for without it we cannot live. Every breath we take throughout our whole life reminds us of that intimate relationship we have with air. Each breath constantly reminds us that we are part of the Source of All That Is and with the whole of life. Our outbreath is cleansing and releases carbon dioxide and impurities. It also contains some of our DNA, which is released on the outbreath. Others breathe it in, so we are all connected through air and breath.

Sylphs are the spirits of the air and they travel with the wind. They have the highest vibration of the four elements. They live for hundreds of years and are said to live on the top of mountains. They vary in size from that of a human to something much smaller. Their work is with the gases and ethers of the earth and one of their functions is to help people with creative inspiration, so they are attracted to people who work with their minds and the creative arts. Some people see them with wings. I can always see them in the clouds: the sky is a scene of constant change.

ACTIVITY: THE HOLY BREATH

Stand outside somewhere where you can feel the breeze or wind. Imagine it is blowing all around you and clearing and cleansing any negativity. See the negativity leaving you in a bubble of light on the breeze.

The spiritual beings of air can transmit healing to you through your breath if you breathe consciously. Through their spiritual energy vibration they can transmit messages by means of pictures, symbols, images, feelings or colours. However you experience them is the means by which they convey their message to you. Their message to you is, 'Breathe in the Holy Breath.' Your breath flows into your chest and your heart and angels, devas and nature spirits meet you in your heart.

BREATHE IN THE HOLY BREATH

Breathe!
Breathe us into your heart,
Which is a palace
For angels.
Its pillars are the petals
Of the rose.
Its altar
Is the diamond-like dewdrop
At the centre of the rose
Scintillating
With all the colours of the rainbow.

Breathe
Into your heart centre.
Centre yourself
Into the rose temple –
The temple of the heart.

Breathe!
And free your thoughts
Free your mind.
Wake up!
Surrender to the freedom of your spirit,
Your spirit that guides you
Life after life.

Breathe!
Follow your hunches,
Follow your feelings,
Your intuition.
Allow your heart to guide you
Along the path of your destiny,
Your chosen path,
Chosen by you before your birth,
That path
Which nourishes your innermost
hopes and dreams.

Breathe!
Build that path
Breath by breath,
Step by step,
By your thoughts and actions
Until your hopes and dreams become
reality.
Build the stepping-stones
Of your vision
Until you reach it.
This is your Path of Freedom.

The colour of air (sky) is blue. Air represents brotherhood and sisterhood and our intellectual abilities. Air beings help us with decision-making, communication, justice and ideals like equality. They can influence the thoughts of humanity as a whole and help to bring about tolerance and respect for everybody. They inspire a deeper intuitive understanding of the oneness behind all creation. They can inspire people with divine wisdom. By attuning to these angels, you can get a better understanding about the deeper meaning behind life's challenges.

Air is obviously closely associated with the breath and being mindful of breath leads one into meditation. In meditation, the breath can take you to deeper and more profound levels of intuitive guidance, the guidance of spirit and the different levels of consciousness.

The air that we breathe and that always surrounds us is invisible, but we can see its effects in the light breezes that cool us when it is hot or in gale-force winds that cause devastation and damage. We cannot live without the breath of life, sometimes called the Holy Breath. We forget that as we breathe in and out of the heart centre we are connecting with the divine. We always love to hear the songs of the birds that bring pleasure on a summer's day or watch the great raptors, birds of prey, as they float effortlessly on the thermal air currents.

The eagle is the greatest bird of all and there are many myths and legends about eagles. The Native Americans regard it as a symbol of Great Spirit, the Source of All That Is. They say that eagle flies higher than any other bird and can hear the messages from Great Spirit and bring them to us in meditation. The eagle's message is that we always have complete access to awesome spiritual power, the power of Great Spirit (God) and the angels. Eagle can take us beyond the earthly life to the stars of the universe. Allow yourself to adventure, let yourself soar and be supported by angels of light. When you feel weighed down with decision-making, eagle helps to see the larger picture.

For a meditation on the archangel Raphael and the Eagle, turn the page.

ARCHANGEL RAPHAEL AND EAGLE MESSAGE AND MEDITATION

Eagle is the power animal for the east and represents the power of Great Spirit, the connection to the Creator, the Source of All That Is. Raphael is the archangel for the east. Eagle reminds us that though we need to remember our connection to the earth, we can keep our vision on the world of light. Of all creatures, eagle flies the highest and is closest to Great Spirit.

Eagle medicine reminds us to draw on strength and courage as we experience the highs and lows of everyday life. In our meditations we can soar with eagle above the ordinary everyday events. We can remember to feed our soul as well as our physical bodies.

What do you do each day for your own enjoyment, relaxation and refreshment? We all need to do simple things, just for us, whether it is sitting in the garden, walking in the park or countryside or the mountains, taking part in a sport, spending time with family and friends, bathing in essential oils or listening to our favourite music. Whatever feeds your soul, do it and then remember the joy, the peace, and the relaxation you felt and radiate it out to the world around you. Share your joy inwardly with the dark places of the world and those who need joy in their lives.

Begin your meditation by sitting comfortably on a chair or on the floor. Begin to observe your breathing. Imagine that you are breathing in and out of the heart chakra for a few minutes until your mind becomes quiet and still.

Now imagine that you are an eagle, soaring high above the earth. Feel the warmth of the sunshine on your wings, feel the air currents supporting you. As you feel the wind, remember that the air is also the power of your breath, your power to breathe in light, health, strength, courage, and wisdom. It is the life-force itself.

Looking down upon the earth, it spreads out below you like a map. The rivers look like silver ribbons as they make their way to the sea. The waters sparkle like jewels in the light of the sun. Even the highest mountains are below you. Eagle brings enlightenment and illumination, the goals of meditation and the gifts of eagle. It gives you permission to follow the path that your heart desires.

Within the etheric planes in the great mountains such as the Himalayas, the Andes and other great mountain chains, exist great temples for devas, angels and ascended masters. They cannot be identified by any modern technology such as satellite as they are invisible to the earthly senses. But in your meditation, become aware of them and the scintillating streams of colour that radiate from the devic temples.

Some mountains are themselves temples of the devas, and the devas gather there. You are more likely to be aware of them when the mountains are still and tranquil and not crowded with tourists. Tuning in to the devas, be aware of their colours, which represent the spiritual qualities of the spectrum that we have already discussed. Breathe in their light and colours and as you breathe out, send them your love and light in return.

Allow yourself to float easily, experiencing the peace and stillness of being high up above the world. Take long breaths of pure, clear air into your lungs, filling yourself with new ideas, with qualities you need right now in your life. Continuing to breathe easily, feel and see yourself being filled with the pure white light of spirit. It quietens your thoughts and feelings and brings you new insights.

Think about anything you want to change in your life. Continue to enjoy the feeling of soaring high above the earth, seeing with new eyes, the eyes of Eagle. Become like the spirit of Eagle and choose to fly in any direction you wish.

As you return from your flight, thank Eagle, the devas and Raphael for the insights you received. Finish your meditation, opening your eyes when you are ready. Write down anything you want to do with your life and decide one thing that will help you to do it, and then begin it.

ANGELS AND BIRDS

Many spiritual traditions consider there is a mystical connection between angels and birds. Ken Carey, who wrote the book THE RETURN OF THE BIRD TRIBES, stated:

'I will tell you also of the gentle tribes from which we come, the tribes whom some now call angels, but who, in simpler days were known by another name. For thousands of gentle circlings around her star, the peoples of the Americas, the Highlanders of Asia, the natives of central Africa and earth people the world over, have known us as The Bird Tribes.'[1]

Carey goes on to say that the bird tribes (angels) have not been present much amongst human beings during historical times (the last two or three thousand years), but are now returning to guide us. The spirit messenger communicating to Carey pointed out that it is time to remember our spiritual origin and attune to the frequencies of world healing, the frequencies of love. Whenever we invite angels to live among us and help us, they will come.

Other messages from birds are seen in the swan, that beautiful graceful bird of the water. It was the messenger of the Celtic underworld. The crane is the bringer of good fortune to the Buddhists. The blackbird was seen by the Celts as the guardian between the two worlds, the one of every day and the spiritual world. In the Koran, angelic, spiritual knowledge is referred to as the language of birds. Doves are considered bringers of peace and are often seen with an olive branch or twig in their beaks. Noah sent out a dove after the great flood and she eventually returned to the ark with an olive twig in her beak. The dove is also seen as a symbol of the Holy Spirit, when a dove descended to Christ at his baptism.

Birds can bring their angelic messages to us in many different ways, not only through their physical presence and sightings. We can receive their messages through meditation, dreams, seeing pictures and photographs or being attracted to poetry and stories. There are several books which describe the spiritual meaning of birds, but I will mention just one more, the robin, which is special to me. At times of stress or special times in my life I have often seen robins. I have always associated robins with the presence of angels. Once, when I was meeting another angel teacher in my home, a robin came up to the open French windows and sang to us. When we met in my friend's home, we sat in the garden, and robins surrounded us and sang.

The red colour of the breast (the heart) of the

robin reflects its life-force and the passion of the heart chakra. It symbolizes spiritual fire (love) and it will act as your guide to the world of angels. The robin's joyful song brings us a feeling of trust and strength. When it is seen at the time of the Winter Solstice and New Year, it brings hope for the future and new life as the seasons turn on. If a robin is your power animal, it signifies the need to sing your own song if you wish for new growth.

Robins lay pale blue eggs. That is the colour of the throat chakra, which helps us to use our own voice, sing our own song and begin anew. Robins may rear more than one brood of young in a year.

*

After writing those paragraphs about the robin, I went into the garden. It had been too cold to go out for quite a while and I hadn't seen any robins. But this morning a flash of movement caught my eye. It moved again! In the azalea's bare branches was a robin. It didn't sing but we looked at each other for a long time. It was as if we were gazing into each other's eyes. Angels always confirm their messages!

Lesley's Story

Lesley's father had suffered bravely from severe arthritis and other illnesses for many years before he died. Lesley felt his death very keenly and was comforted by the daily walks she took in the local park with her black Labrador, Lucky. She had many doggy walking friends.

They noticed that a robin with a redbreast and yellow wings kept flying around them. They were surprised to see a robin with unusually yellow wings. Lesley's father always liked to wear a yellow sweater, so she realized that the robin was a sign from her father, an angel, letting her know that he was always with her and she didn't need to be sad. He was happy to be released from his old and ailing body.

Chapter Four

THE ANGELS AND DEVAS OF FIRE AND LIGHT

'Just as a candle cannot burn without fire, men cannot live without a spiritual life.'

Buddha

THE ELEMENT FIRE deals with our ideals and inspirations. Fire helps with our career, enthusiasms, love of adventure and travel, and self-development. It has the power to create and destroy more than any of the other elements. It is symbolic of the spirit and of life itself. Passion, creativity and enthusiasm are all part of the fire element. We talk about 'firing up' our imagination. There is a lot more symbolism about fire: think of the Olympic Torch, which represents the aspirations and the peaceful coming together of the nations. In Acts of the Apostles in the New Testament, the Holy Spirit is seen as tongues of flame.

Many traditions use fire to dispose of dead bodies. Flames and smoke carry the spirit to heaven and also cleanse and purify the remains. In the ancient Celtic tradition, at Beltane (May 1st) cattle were driven between bonfires to protect them from disease. The Great Fire of London in 1666 wiped out most of the city, but it wiped out the terrible plague that preceded it. Then it became possible to rebuild a much better city, the basis of the one we see today.

Salamanders are fire sprites that are the spiritual essence of the fire element and without them fire could not exist. They are obedient to the devas. Some people see them as small flames or balls of light. If you have ever watched the flames of a bonfire, you may have seen small sparks flying into the air. They are the salamanders. They are present even in the smallest flame, like that of a match or even a spark. I have watched the flame of a candle seem to 'dance' in time to the music that is playing. Make sure there is no draught if you want to try this. If the candle flame dances too vigorously, quieten your thoughts and breathe quietly and smoothly, requesting the flame to be still.

A friend, Mark, sits in a meditation group in which the sitters influence the movement of the candle flame with their thoughts. This works and demonstrates how the power of thought

ANGEL OF THE SUN

I am Sol, the Great Sun,
Source of all your strength and life,
Of upliftment and joy
I send my angels of light
Bringing warmth and nourishment
To your world
And to you.

As you relax in my warm rays
My life force energy
Is absorbed into you,
Body, mind and spirit.

There is an angel
For each of my rays

And they bring the light
I send you.

My light is your nourishment
That also nourishes
The flowers, vegetables and grains,
Salads and fresh foods you love to eat.

I send my light
And you feel lighter
And full of energy
Though the clouds may hide me
I still shine on
In your heart
And my angels of light
Walk beside you.

can influence the natural world. In other words, it is a demonstration of the so-called law of attraction. They are greatly affected by human thought and bad temper can cause fire sprites to be mischievous, although, like children, they don't understand the results of their actions.

In Greek myth, fire symbolized the wisdom that separated divinity (the gods) from humans.

Prometheus stole fire from the gods and showed the courage needed to challenge the laws of the gods. The sun bathes the earth in its light and energy and without it there would be no life on earth. Within the sun there is a spiritual sun, as there is with every physical form, for it is the spirit which is divine, which is life.

'Love is the first cause of all life. Love is light and

heat and life itself.' *White Eagle*[1]

The Egyptian pharaoh Akhenaten had a vision of the One God, Aten, as the sun, with rays of light shining in every direction. This is depicted as a shrine stela depicting Akhenaten and his wife Nefertiti and their daughters are shown as a family worshipping, the Aten depicted as the sun. A hand is shown in blessing at the end of each ray.

The colours of fire are red, orange and yellow and are associated with the lower three chakras,

MEDITATION WITH ANGELS AND NATURE SPIRITS OF SUNLIGHT

Begin your meditation by sitting quietly and tuning in to your breathing. If you can do this out of doors, take a few moments to look around you at the beauty of nature. If indoors, close your eyes and create a special place with your creative imagination, which is the beginning of clairvoyance. Visualize the sun shining brightly over you. (If you are outside, don't stare at the sun.)

Feel the rays of the sun envelop you like a pyramid of light. Visualize an angel in each ray of the sun, sharing this light with you. Breathe in the light that surrounds you and feel yourself being filled with a sense of peace, love and tranquillity, a feeling of total relaxation. Remember a time in your life, when you were carefree and totally happy and at peace. As you relive this memory, feel yourself once again filled with that feeling of peace, love, joy and serenity. As you continue to visualize the sunlight filling you and surrounding

you, visualize your heart chakra at the centre of your chest. Your spiritual heart centre begins to shine like a sun.

Gradually the light grows bigger and bigger, and radiates out. It fills the place where you are sitting and then grows larger and larger, to fill your home and the people in it, your town or city, your workplace, your country and then the whole planet, sharing that sense of peace, serenity and tranquillity with everyone.

Spend some time in this space of deep peace. Then, when you feel the meditation is complete, visualize the sunlight in your heart centre grow smaller and smaller until it becomes like a small flame, dissolve the visualization and bring your awareness back to your breath, then your physical body. Open your eyes and make sure you are grounded again. Have a drink of water, move about and return to your everyday activities.

which enable people to connect with the energy of the earth. Although the base of the spine chakra, *muladhara*, is associated with the element of earth in the yoga tradition, it is also the seat of *kundalini* energy, divine love. By living a good life *kundalini* is transmuted to spiritual energy. The angels, devas and nature spirits of fire bring love, strength and vitality, and a feeling of moving on. They are very inspirational and inspire creativity. They are radiant, like the bright sunlight of a summer day. Fire represents *unconditional love*.

These angels enfold you in divine unconditional love and fill you with confidence and leadership qualities as well as a pioneering spirit and love of adventure. Sometimes this adventurousness can lead to 'hot-headedness' and getting carried away with enthusiasm, and then people wear themselves out. They need to learn to pace themselves, or they can suffer headaches or nervous problems.

The human spirit is a spark of the divine fire, that spark of the divine hidden in the heart chakra, the divine love that radiates into the heart itself. The most spiritual function of the heart chakra is unconditional love and also the reception of the divine will. You might describe someone as 'warm-hearted' when this aspect of spirituality is open to the light, to *fire*. When the heart chakra opens wider through the practice of meditation and yoga

or other spiritual practices, there is no room for narrowmindedness or prejudice. The soul lesson of the fire element is love and attunement to beings of fire brings about a feeling of deepest love.

Picture the way in which flames burn up all that is old and unwanted, to bring in new conditions. After a forest fire, new plants spring up almost overnight, as though they have just been waiting for the right conditions to allow their growth. Consider how fire can bring warmth and energy in the coldest winter. All of these pictures demonstrate the different energies of fire. Fire brings a great feeling of warmth and vitality and new energy. It provides enthusiasm for new plans

ACTIVITY: BURNING IT ALL AWAY

Picture bright, fiery flames leaping up towards the heavens, burning away old clutter and all that is no longer needed in your life. Think of any thoughts, feelings or problems going into the flames and burning them away, bringing new energies and qualities that you need to move on. Visualize angelic beings and salamanders that look like leaping flames. They inspire you to release old unwanted 'inner stuff' that you no longer need, causing deep cleansing of the soul and allowing yourself the freedom to change.

If you have any old memories or upsets, and have a safe place to burn paper, write down the memories or draw or doodle them, then burn them in a flame. I have used an old large saucepan I no longer cook with to do this out in the garden. On a workshop I attended, we were able to have a large bonfire in the grounds. Everyone drew a large illustration of issues they wanted to release, using flipchart paper. Then we went outside and everyone in turn spoke aloud the things they wished to release and put the paper illustration onto the bonfire. It was fascinating to watch, as I could really see the fire sprites leaping up into the air and carrying away all the old unwanted memories and experiences.

and ideas. Angels use the element of fire to 'burn up' the old to make way for the new. You could say these angels are angels of transformation.

Some affirmations for working with the fire element are

• I am divine power
• I am divine joy
• I am divine creativity
• I am divine inspiration
• I am filled with inspiration from the light of the sun
• My heart overflows with divine love
• I aspire to the highest I can achieve
• I am open to divine, loving wisdom
• I am filled with divine, loving energy and strength that transforms my life in perfect and harmonious ways.

THE PHOENIX

When I was attuning to angels of fire I had a very clear meditation about a phoenix. It is said to be part eagle and part pheasant. The one shown opposite is from a manuscript called the Aberdeen Bestiary. There are myths and legends from all over the world about the phoenix. According to the apocryphal Book of Enoch, phoenixes are birdlike angels of equal rank with the seraphim and cherubim. The phoenix symbolizes alchemy, the spiritualization of matter. Some legends state that it sets itself on fire every hundred years, others that it may live for over a thousand years. After three days it is reborn from the ashes, representing resurrection, ascension and immortality and the indestructibility of the human spirit. It also represents a period of time. Some say that there is only one

phoenix in existence at any time and that its true home is in paradise. Another legend about it is that it is symbolic of the dying of the sun as it slips over the horizon at nightfall.

My understanding of the phoenix is that it is a messenger from the angels and devas of fire, and it gave me the message below.

Illustration from the 12th Century Aberdeen Bestiary (Public Domain)

THE PHOENIX

I am Phoenix
With robes of red and gold
Radiating with streams of colour
Like feathers of flame
Flashing all around me
And connecting with you
Whenever you need to change.
You change and transform
As you move up the spiral of life.
Spiralling from each strand of your DNA
You move
From being a simple cell
To a sun, a galaxy, a universe.
I am Phoenix,

The Age reborn
I supervise the next thousand years
With my angel helpers
The Angels of Fire
Then I transform and am born again
From the flames
Of rebirth.

I bring you a Golden Feather.
Use it for your inspiration
To create, to write, to draw, to paint.
See its magic bring new life to your ideas
As you co-create with the Great Creator,
he Source of All That Is.

THE SERAPHIM

The highest and most splendid of the choirs of angels are the seraphim. Seraphim are the closest to God and are said to surround Him and continually sing glorious songs. Some people have been lucky enough to hear their music and say it is like no other heard on Earth.

My mother had an angel vision on the night my father passed into Spirit. She said she heard heavenly music, the like of which she had never heard before or since.

Like a waterfall, their songs cascade right down through all the angel hierarchies, forming a continuous creative song of divine, loving energy, the fire of spiritual love, which never ceases throughout all eternity. All angels are filled with divine love. It is their mission to surround everything and everyone with this beautiful song of creation. Their name means 'fiery burning ones'. This fire is not the painful burning fire of hell, but the passionate flame of divine love. Seraphim are said to be so bright that no one would be able to look at them. They were the angels seen by Isaiah in his vision (Isaiah 6:1-7), which records:

'Above him were seraphs, each with six wings: With two wings they covered their faces, with two they covered their feet and with two they were

> ## WE ARE THE SERAPHIM
>
> We are the seraphim.
> We are living flame, fire of love.
> We are the living, redemptive flame of love.
> We pour out this ever-living flame of adoration
> Singing 'Holy, holy, holy is the Lord of Hosts.
> Heaven and Earth are full of His Glory.
> Sanctus, Ssanctus, sanctus, Dominus Deus Sabaoth'.

flying. And they were calling to one another: Holy, holy, holy is the Lord Almighty; the whole earth is full of his glory.' In his vision, Isaiah saw a seraph touch his lips with a hot coal to purify him to prepare him for his work as a prophet.

In his book, ANGELS: AN ENDANGERED SPECIES, Malcolm Godwin speculates that the song of the seraphim is a song of creation, a song of celebration. The seraphim are beings of pure light.[1]

FIRE AND LIGHT MEDITATION WITH SERAPHIEL, PRINCE OF THE SERAPHIM

Sit or Stand in any comfortable position.

Focus on your breath. Notice the expansion and contraction of the upper abdomen, chest and lungs as the breath comes and goes. Continue to notice every breath, allow the breath to breathe you. You begin to feel calm and centred.

Visualize yourself inside an immense six-pointed star of light. It begins above your head and extends all around you and beneath your feet. At the apex of the star overhead you see an immense crystal diamond light, like liquid crystal. This is your connection to spirit, the Source of All That Is, the Stellar Gateway. It sparkles like a diamond, with all the colours of the spectrum, even though it appears to be clear and transparent.

Beneath your feet, at the point of the descending triangle of the star, you see a beautiful crystal, your earth star chakra. It is black tourmaline. Our creative ideas and expression always begin in the dark, like the unborn child in the darkness of the womb or a seed held in the warm darkness of the earth to await germination. The Stellar Gateway and the Earth Star keep you balanced and aligned in matter, between Heaven and Earth.

Raise your hands above your head and call on Seraphiel to connect you with the crystal star, the celestial fire of your Stellar Gateway chakra. As you breathe in, visualize sparkling fire and light filling your whole being and radiating from your heart, hands and feet. You are filled and radiating fire and light, spiritual love. You are a six-pointed star or flower of light.

Continue breathing in sparkling fire and light until you wish to conclude. Bring your attention back to your breath and close your chakras by visualizing each of them like a flower. Close each chakra by seeing the flower close its petals.

Seraphiel is described as the prince of the Seraphim. 'His face is like the face of angels and his body is like the body of eagles.' He teaches the other seraphim how to sing God's praises. His body is full of countless sparkling eyes, each as bright as the morning star.

Many archangels are named as being of the order of seraphim: Michael, Seraphiel, Gabriel, and Metatron. Archangel Metatron is considered to have been Enoch, the ancestor of Noah, who ascended. In Genesis 5:24 we read: 'And Enoch walked with God, and he was not, for God took him.'

Mystics throughout the ages have thought that certain people are taken straight to heaven after death. St John is said to have ascended thus, like the Virgin Mary. Melchizedek is said to have become an angel after death.

The widow of Rumi, the Sufi poet, had a vision of him after death 'winged as a seraph'.[1]

Chapter Five

THE ANGELS AND DEVAS OF WATER

Water, being the first element, has a wonderful power
and possesses wonderful properties on the spiritual
and on the etheric plane. The water angels of the
universe are connected with the water element in your
own nature and also with your emotional reactions.
They bring harmony and create peace and order.

WHITE EAGLE'S LITTLE BOOK OF ANGELS,

MANY OF OUR creation myths speak of a time when the earth rose out of a watery ocean from which all life was created. It was in a sense formless: water has no form of its own but takes the shape of its container. It can freeze into ice or evaporate into steam and condensation. It can fall from the sky as rain or form mist and fog. Subject to the law of gravity, it flows downwards from its highest point until it reaches the sea. Early settlements and civilizations were built beside rivers or seas – such is the need for water for cleansing, drinking and agriculture. Most cultures talk of a great flood that once purified the planet and all inhabitants.

UNDINES

Undines are the elementals of water. They can control the course and function of the water element. They live within the water and cannot usually be seen with normal vision as they are constantly flowing and moving with the action of the water. They are thought to be the origin of legends about mermaids. Their colours are all the colours of water, from blue to green and all the shades from the palest to the deepest, as well as clear. When still and calm enough it reflects its surroundings like a mirror.

Overleaf is a mindfulness visualization to quieten mental chatter that helps to make a clearer connection to undines and devas of water. This visualization involves picturing yourself floating on water. If you have any fears or concern about being in or on water, omit this and choose another visualization.

It is necessary to control our emotions, and water, like all the elements, can reflect human emotions for better or worse . Undines live

A MINDFULNESS VISUALIZATION

Choose a time when you have been in a stressful situation. Picture yourself floating on your back in a pool of water or in the ocean.

You are quite safe in or on the water. It will not harm you. Like all bodies of water it has movement and you feel yourself rising and falling with the gentle current. Breathe in and feel yourself gently moving up with the water. Breathe out, and the surface of the water also moves down. Slowly your breathing becomes deeper and calmer and the movement of the water also becomes still and calm.

When you feel ready, come out of the water in your mind, have a good stretch and breathe more deeply. Visualize roots from the soles of your feet connecting you to earth again.

in rock pools and marshland and they like underwater caves. They work with underwater plants; small undines live under leaves of water plants like water lilies, and under lotus flowers. They are present in everything that contains water – and that includes human beings, as most of our body is formed of water or liquid and our cells function in a liquid medium.

Do you like to watch the reflections of the light on the waves and the tide as you sit by the sea on a sunny day? Once, when I did this, I saw the water sprites dancing over the surface of the water. One Easter we were staying in Bournemouth and I really became aware of the angels, undines and other nature spirits of the elements. The weather had been intensely cold with flakes of snow, but Easter Sunday was bright and sunny. We took the opportunity to rush down to the front, where we sat on a seat, relaxed, and enjoyed the sunshine.

There had been a full moon on the Saturday evening, but now the sun was shining on the sea and the tide was coming in. I watched the sunshine reflecting off the waves. The light took the form of a great deva of light, the landscape deva for the area. Suddenly I saw hundreds of water sprites (undines) and fire sprites (salamanders) in a dance of joy and celebration for the resurrection of the Sun (Son). Far out to sea began a procession of silvery 'liquid' sprites as the rays of the sun caught the water and the fire sprites danced on the surface. The salamanders and undines began a procession on the path of the tide as it approached the land. Hundreds and thousands were marching together. They separated and came together again in a dance of harmony and light.

They looked like stars of light, making a pattern

OPENING YOUR VISION TO THE UNDINES AND WATER SPRITES

A traditional Eastern visualization to develop inner vision is to create or remember somewhere you have seen water lilies or lotus flowers. If you have difficulty remembering, you may like to use the one below. If you are lucky enough to visit a park or botanical garden where they grow and it is a safe place to sit and close your eyes, you can practise this visualization.

Picture the roots of the water lily sitting in the mud of the bottom of the pool or lake. The mud is dirty and dark but provides nourishment for the roots. It is in the darkness and safety that all living things begin to grow. The roots are nourished and begin to send up a stem that reaches upwards towards the light and warmth of the sun. The water becomes clearer and at last the stem reaches the surface of the water. It sends out leaves that spread onto the surface of the lake. They live on the surface of the water but don't get wet as they have waxy leaves. Slowly, lotus flower buds begin to form and open to *light* and become full blossoms.

on the water. The colours were like molten silver and blue and formed patterns like old-fashioned folk dances and circle dances. Salamanders partnered undines as they danced onto the land to celebrate the Resurrection, the full moon with the sun in Aries, the incoming of the tide, and the marriage of the four elements, water and earth, fire and air. As the water reached the beach, water and fire sprites leapt into the air and the procession continued, a celebration of joy beginning far out to sea and coming in to the land on the path of the sun and the tide. We sat there for nearly an hour, drinking in an experience we knew would always live in our memories.

ARCHANGEL GABRIEL AND
THE POWER OF WATER

Water is able to reflect its surroundings like a mirror. The moon controls and rules the tides and is considered to be feminine, as a foetus is supported by water in its mother's womb before birth. Traditionally, Archangel Gabriel rules the moon. If you can sit by the sea to do it, the meditation in the next column may take on a greater reality for you.

To understand the power of water, visualize the earth as seen from space, as it has been photographed many times now by satellites and space missions. Like ourselves it is largely formed of water. See what a beautiful blue jewel it is, sparkling and radiating the light from its watery surface. Water nurtures us and we need to drink plenty of water. It is nourishing and cleansing and we feel purified and renewed after bathing or showering.

People love to go to the sea or the ocean and sit by the water. It is soothing to listen to the waves gently swishing to and fro as they slide up the sand and roll back to the sea on a still, hot, summer's day. Like all the elements, too much water is destructive, but it enables people to build anew. It is purifying and transforming. Water also

Visualize the ocean or sit beside it if you have the opportunity. The tide is coming in and the early morning sun is shining across the sea, making a path of light from the sun to you. As you look into the light, the path of light takes the form of a magnificent deva.

Its aura is all light and as you look into it you can see rainbow colours, translucent and pure. It constantly moves with the movement of the water and the reflections of the light. The waves seem to start far out to sea and you can see little lights reflecting on the water. They move nearer and nearer to the shore and begin to take on the form of little elemental beings, like salamanders and undines. At the same time, there are also small flashes of fire like tiny flames from the fire sprites of the sun.

Visualize the great water deva, with the elementals, nature spirits, of the water, fire, air and earth dancing together to celebrate the new life of the spring equinox. Feel joy and enthusiasm in yourself at the thought of warm weather, longer days and more light returning and bringing a burst of renewed life to flowers and birds, insects and butterflies. The nature spirits work with the devas and angels to build the form of all creation.

ARCHANGEL GABRIEL

I AM Gabriel
Winged with moonlight.
Each feathered vibration
Mirrors the subtle colours
Of moonstone, opal and pearl,
The subtle energies from the moon,
The seas and oceans
Of planet Earth.

Seek my colours
Within the seashells of the planet,
Oyster, abalone, mother-of-pearl.

Like the ocean itself
There are hidden treasures.
Seek what is hidden
For the search is worthwhile.

Then envision
The subtle colours of my wings
As they flash in the sunlight
Like white peacock feathers
Bejewelled at each feathery tip.
My robe is white linen,
My girdle is gold!

helps us to cleanse ourselves from negative energy that we have taken in from other people or places and to dive deeply into our emotions and feelings and the world of our unconscious.

Rain is a concern of the deva of water. It is a very precious resource that we cannot live without. Can we love the rain? In the UK we get very tired of constant rain but in some countries people dance for joy when it rains. The teacher

White Eagle says,

'Never grumble about the rain, never grumble about the air currents and the wind, even if it is uncomfortable and buffets you. We speak of your spiritual life as well as your physical. Welcome the brothers and sisters of the air; welcome the brothers of the sun.'[1]

THE MAGIC OF WATER

When I was in Egypt, a tour guide said it rained once in Luxor during the twentieth century and people went out to look at it and feel it! Drinking water is so precious for our health. Dr Masaru Emoto, author of many books about his research into the secret messages in water, apparently demonstrated that water carries healing powers when you place a message of love, light, healing and peace on a glass or jug of water. I put quartz crystals in my water filters and write loving, healing messages with felt pen on the outside of the jug. People comment on the sweet taste of the water.

I also grow orchids, which I usually buy when they are reduced in price at the local supermarket! Some of my orchids have flowered for several years and people ask me how I do it when theirs die off after a few weeks. I think if Emoto's theories are true, then the messages written on the water filters encourage healthy plant growth.

HOMEOPATHY

The development of Homeopathy is credited to Samuel Hahnemann (1755–1843). He developed a system of treatment based on 'like treats like'. Homeopathy remains controversial as it has not been systematically investigated by the scientific and medical community. One area where it has been said to work demonstrably is by homeopathic veterinary practitioners, who claim animals cannot experience the placebo effect so when healed by homeopathy it can be ascribed to the homeopathic treatment.

BACH FLOWER REMEDIES

Edward Bach (1886–1936), whom we met earlier (p. 43), trained as a medical doctor and worked in the field of bacteriology in chronic disease. His research led him to believe that personality types and illness were connected. He worked with vaccines and then with homeopathic principles until he began to experiment with flower remedies. In 1930 he gave up his successful medical practice to concentrate on a search for safe plants and trees that had a healing effect. He published a book called THE TWELVE HEALERS AND OTHER REMEDIES. He discovered that each flower reflected a negative emotional state. Bach prepared essences by soaking a safe herb or flower in pure spring water in sunshine. Bach flower remedies are still in use today all over the world.[1]

In other continents with different plants from

Europe, several practitioners have developed more remedies.

Following this discussion about homeopathy and flower remedies, I hope it can be said that water carries memory. So we see how vital it is for people to use positive thought and attunement to help nature spirits to heal the Earth.

Water not only washes us, it also purifies and cleanses Gaia, planet Earth.

The water element, as I've said, is associated with our emotional body, our emotions; it is also part of the emotions of the planet. This emotional vehicle reflects the pain and suffering which form our thoughts, feelings, actions and beliefs. The terrible pollution in the oceans, seas and rivers reflects this chaos of thoughts and feelings. Sea creatures like turtles think plastic bags are jellyfish and eat them, which causes a slow, agonizing death. It has now been discovered through post-mortem examinations of dead sea mammals and other sea creatures that there is an accumulation of plastic waste products in their stomachs and gut that most certainly contributes to their death.

The following news item is from the London *Evening Standard*.

DEAD WHALE HAD 40KG OF PLASTIC IN STOMACH

A dead whale that washed up in the Philippines had 40kg of plastic bags in its stomach. Workers at D'Bone Collector Museum recovered the Cuvier's beaked whale east of Daveo City. A post-mortem examination suggested it died from 'gastric shock' after ingesting all the plastic. It included sixteen rice sacks, four banana plantation bags and multiple shopping bags.

The whale was found on the shores of Barangay Cadunan in the municipality of Mabini on Friday. In a Facebook post, the museum said 'the animal was filled with the most plastic we have ever seen in a whale.[1]

There are areas of ocean where this plastic and marine rubbish has collected rather like an island. One such is a collection of plastic and floating rubbish found in the north and central Pacific Ocean.[2] In the same week as the story about the dead whale, though, there was a news item in *Positive News* magazine about hundreds of people who took part in the UK's first supermarket plastic mass 'unwrap'.[3]

There are many places in the world with sacred springs and wells where people go to have cures. A famous one is at Lourdes, in France. It is well known for several appearances of Mother Mary, Our Lady of Lourdes, to a peasant girl, Bernadette Soubirous, in 1858. Lourdes has since developed into a major pilgrimage centre for Roman Catholics, and during the season from March to October Lourdes can accommodate five million visitors. Mother Mary is also known as the Queen of the Angels. The River

Ganges in India is also said to be a sacred river and Hindus flock to bathe in it and to be cleansed of sins. It is considered to be the heart of Indian culture and is named after the Goddess Ganga. London has twenty sacred wells and their names can often be discovered by place names, such as Sadler's Wells, the famous theatre, Clerkenwell, Camberwell, Muswell (Hill) and Hanwell.

White Eagle talks often of the stilling of the storm on the Sea of Galilee as a case of 'the Master' in the heart arising and taking charge, just as Jesus did. He said once, 'those devas and great ones who control the powers of nature dare not refuse that mind which had attained the power of mastery'.

ACTIVITY: WASHING STRESS AWAY

After a stressful day, splash your face and hands with water and sprinkle drops of water over your head. If you have time, stand in the shower and feel the water washing away all stressful thoughts and feelings. See these as dirty water washing down the drain and taking all negativity away.

THE SOUL LESSON OF THE WATER ELEMENT

The soul lesson of the water element is peace and attunement to angels of water brings about deep peace. Picture water in all its many aspects, from ocean waves, great waterfalls, tumbling rivers, tiny streams, early morning dew on the plants and flowers, to the still waters of a peaceful lake that reflects the surroundings just like a mirror. All of these pictures demonstrate the different moods of water. Our emotions can be just like this, from a raging storm to a peaceful lake. Angels of the water element help us to master our emotions instead of us being mastered by them. It has a cleansing aspect to its quality. Water also assists us to flow with life.

Affirmations for angels of water:
- I am centred and still
- I am peaceful and filled with joy
- Clarity and peace fill my heart and mind
- I breathe in peace. I breathe out all worry and tension
- Angels help me to create my inner sanctuary of peace.

Angelic qualities of water are peace, tolerance, power, constancy, reflection, and stillness.

Since the research about the healing power of water that was done by Masaru Emoto, the

ACTIVITY: THE PEACEFUL LAKE

Imagine a peaceful still lake like the one on the opposite page. It is like a mirror, reflecting the scenes around it and the sky above. In the same way, the calm soul reflects the Source of All-That-Is.

Japanese researcher, we have all become more aware of the importance of water at a deeper spiritual healing level. Emoto discovered how to photograph water crystals. He also discovered that using powerful prayers over water changed the crystal. When hateful words and mantras were used, the crystals became ugly and malformed.

The cells of our bodies are formed largely of water and we need to drink plenty of pure water daily to remain healthy. Writing prayers and healing mantras on water filters and bottles of water creates healing properties in our water. You can also 'draw' a simple shape (called a *yantra* in the yoga tradition), like a star or cross in a circle, or the Sanskrit AUM, with your finger on the surface of the bathwater or chant prayers and mantras in your bath or shower to improve health.

We can also use our ability to visualize in using water imagery to heal planet Earth. Many people used prayer and meditation to help in the Gulf of

Mexico oil spill crisis of 2010.

Water as an element includes all liquids and fluids, and our meditations can include rivers and streams, rain, the sap in trees and the early morning dew of plants, as well as blood and fluids in the human body. We become aware of the connection between the liquids and fluids of the planet and of the body. The angel of water causes the rain to fall where there is drought, and fills the wells and reservoirs. She enters the bloodstream through the cool refreshing pure water that we drink, cleansing and revitalizing our blood. As we bathe or shower each day, she cleanses the body so that we feel clean and fresh. She is the Water of Life.

The ancient Zoroastrians saw the angel of water, Anahita, as a beautiful female angel. She oversaw all the waters of the earth because of its importance for all life. She is depicted as wearing a golden crown and decorated with one hundred stars, a gold-coloured robe and a pitcher of water.

Water reminds us to flow with life. Try to get into the habit of drinking a glass of pure water first thing in the morning and throughout the day.

Affirm:

I am drinking the water of life

As you perform your daily shower or bath, you can also visualize yourself being bathed in the waters of eternal life.

MEDITATION: BATHE IN LIFEGIVING WATERS

Visualize yourself in a beautiful garden. Beside you is a sparkling fountain. As the light catches the spray of water, it vibrates with light and colour. The water falls into a pool, edged with blue aquamarine crystals and tiles. Anahita, the Angel of Water, stands beside it. Her colours are all shades of blue, green and silver. She is so clear and pure she seems almost transparent, yet you can see her form. She gives you a crystal goblet of the water to drink.

As you drink, you are filled with energy, vitality and enthusiasm for your day. Every atom and cell of your whole being radiates with health and vitality. You step into the fountain and its life-giving water and light fill you and surround you with health. Anahita invites you to bathe in the pool if you wish. Feel the cleansing and life-giving waters flowing around you. As you bathe, or shower in the fountain, affirm:

I am bathing in the waters of life.

All your fears and worries are cleansed away in the water and you feel refreshed and renewed. Your blood circulation is filled with life-giving energy and you understand the connection between your bloodstream and the life-giving waters of the planet.

Chapter Six

ANGELS OF ETHER

ETHER, OR SPACE, is considered to be Spirit, the Holy Spirit or the Holy Breath, Breath of God. It is also referred to as Light. In the yoga tradition it is referred to as *prana*. In the Kaushitaki Upanishad, we read,

'Prana is the essence of the life breath.
And what is the life breath?
It is pure consciousness.
And what is pure consciousness?
It is the life breath.'

The English word for breath does not give us the full message of what the breath is. In the Sanskrit word *prana*, the root is *an*, which signifies not only our own breath, but the breath of the universe, the life-force. In Taoism, the term is *chi* (*qi*); the Hebrew term is *ruach* and the Greek is *pneuma*. All of these terms signify that breath is more than the contents of the air we breathe, but the actual life-force, or breath of God. The teacher White Eagle has this to say about breathing and the breath:

'There is much to learn about the art of breathing, which can control your life, your unfoldment and your health on the physical, mental and spiritual planes.'[1]

He goes on to say that when we breathe in, we should imagine we are breathing in light and life. We are not only inhaling air, but we are filling every particle of our being with God's breath. This will help us to forget the difficulties of the physical body and earthly difficulties.

Ether interpenetrates the four physical elements of earth, air, fire and water. It can be experienced through the sixth sense, the intuitive or psychic sense. It is through this sense that, through meditation, or inner vision (clairvoyance) that all angels and devas can be experienced. Therefore because the Holy Breath is the Creator of all, the First Cause, the angels interpenetrate the element of ether in an ocean of consciousness, subsequently the whole universe is contained and contains all sentient beings, the angelic and archangelic kingdoms, devas, elementals and nature spirits and all that is.

Chapter Seven

THE ANGELS AND DEVAS OF THE ELEMENTS AND SPIRITUAL INITIATIONS

WE SAW EARLIER how many of the world's spiritual traditions hold the vision of ultimate union – at-one-ment – with the Creator, the Source of All That Is. There are many names and terms for God and each person has their own favourite. Another one I like to use is Great Mystery, a Native American term, which implies there are many mysteries in life, which we are still trying to solve. In the very beginning of life, before there was a physical world and universe, it is said that God, the Source, created spirits as sparks of light. Through many aeons of time, the sparks or spirits of light developed into more and more dense forms.

'Once spirit comes down to dwell in the flesh, it starts to create what is called a soul, for soul is that part of man's (sic) being which is built up through experiences undergone by the tender inner self of man during incarnation.'[1]

White Eagle

ALCHEMY

Another aspect of ether and spiritual initiation is alchemy. In one respect alchemy was the medieval forerunner to chemistry. In the Middle Ages, it was thought that a combination of the four elements, (earth, air, fire and water) could produce precious metals like gold. Yet this was also a secret code, or metaphor. It meant that the human body (earth) could be transmuted into a precious spiritual substance, gold, representing spiritual development. However, in the European Middle Ages, the Church was in control of what people thought and said. The Inquisition had eyes and ears everywhere so the alchemists hid their researches by disguising them as '(al)chemical' investigations and formulas. So alchemy in that sense was aimed at purifying and perfecting the physical body and discovering a universal cure for disease. Another definition is that it is a synonym for the means of transformation.

Another form of alchemy is taking something ordinary and turning it into something extraordinary, like making an art display using scrap metal. Some beautiful wooden sculptures are also carved from dead branches and tree trunks, which can be seen in parks and gardens. So art can be considered alchemy.

If we consider plants, Paracelsus, in the sixteenth century, maintained that the main role of alchemy was to extract the healing properties of plants. He felt that the distillation process released the most spiritual essences of the plants.

An important aspect of living on Earth is to try to ensure that we eat pure foods, organic if available. Eating and food absorption is also an alchemical process. By cooperating with the devas and nature Sspirits, people can also work to keep Gaia, Mother Earth, purer. Herbs, essential oils and other forms of natural medicines like flower remedies work best when they are pure, grow in the best environment and are protected from pollution.

Thus we can all become alchemists. Through what seems like the heaviness and challenges of daily life Earth's apparent darkness can be transformed into light. By knowing darkness as well as light (gold) we are able to experience transformation.

ANGELS AND TRANSFORMATION

When we are faced with big changes in our lives the angels of transformation will be there to help us. Transformation is an opportunity to change for the better. A well-known Chinese curse goes, 'May you live in interesting times'. We certainly seem to!

The angels remind us that even though we are surrounded by challenges, if we can remember to keep centred in the heart chakra, we can gain strength and master the challenges.

BRAINSTORM

Choose an issue or project that is challenging or you are thinking about. It might be some dilemma you are struggling to work out. Choose a topic such as:

Family/Relationships

Work

A project you want to start

Brainstorm all the pros and cons about it in two columns.

WORKING WITH THE ANGEL OF TRANSFORMATION

MEDITATION

Here is a meditation that came to me from the angel of transformation, the butterfly angel.

Choose the topic you have brainstormed.

Close your eyes. Begin your meditation by breathing gently. Notice how the air flows smoothly in and out. Notice how the lungs, ribs and chest move to the rhythm of the breath. Butterflies are connected to the Air Element, which works with the power of thought. When you feel centred and balanced, think about the idea you chose.

Is it at the beginning? (The egg stage)

Do you need to make a decision about it? (The caterpillar)

You are doing the cocoon stage now, as you go within to meditate.

Are you ready to share your ideas with others? (The butterfly)

When you have gone through all your possibilities and decided which stage of the idea or project you are doing, visualize a beautiful temple. It is like a Greek temple, with pillars of beautiful translucent crystal gemstones. The sun shines on them and they sparkle with many colours, like butterflies in the sunshine. It is the temple of transformation. There are butterflies flying around the outside.

Go inside and you find a room with seats. There are huge vases of flowers around the walls. Sit in one of the seats and invite the angel of transformation to sit beside you. Visualize her beautiful colours. Her companions are the devas of colour and the nature spirits. Remembering the interpretations of the four elements and of the fifth, ether, in earlier sections, you could decide which of the nature spirits or devas would be relevant for you to work with. Then mentally talk to the angel and tell her about your idea, challenge or dilemma. She spreads her many coloured wings and asks you what colour you are drawn to. Tell her. Here are some clues about the meaning of colours.

Red – be grounded and firm

Orange – be creative

Yellow – use more light or use your spiritual wisdom

Green – be adaptable and harmonious

Blue – work with helpful affirmations

Indigo – use your intuition

Violet – cleanse yourself and the situation with the violet flame and work with your higher self.

Visualize yourself being surrounded and filled with the colour you see. Continue to talk to the angel until you get some ideas about what you might do. Then visualize yourself putting your ideas into practice. Continue the meditation or repeat it until you become clear about what you need to do. Then thank the angel and say goodbye, as you leave the temple of transformation.

You find yourself once again sitting in your room. Breathe gently until you are ready to open your eyes. When you can, write down your ideas from the meditation in your journal. This helps to ground your ideas so you can put them into practice. Write the first thing you plan to do.

A RESUMÉ OF THE FOUR ELEMENTS

So we have seen that the physical body is the densest one, and thus gives us the experiences that help us to grow and develop our talents and gifts and a more spiritual understanding of life. Each of the experiences of the four elements described has angelic beings that are with us as we undergo significant experiences, which can be described as initiations. So the water initiation involves mastering emotions, feelings and desires, so that we no longer drift like flotsam on the river from one emotion to another in the turmoil of our feelings. We reach a stage when we think we have overcome all our raging anger or suffering and will experience it no more. Then comes a time of testing, when we are confronted again with our old demons and need to deal with them.

Gabriel, the archangel of *water*, stands beside us giving strength and confidence that we can overcome our deepest fears again. We learn to become as still as that peaceful lake which mirrors its surroundings and enables us to hear the voice of the angel and of our higher self, our soul. Archangel Gabriel is considered to be the Angel of the Moon, which rules water. The tides are fuller at the time of the full moon and the moon is considered feminine, and so connected with birth

A MESSAGE FROM
THE ANGEL OF TRANSFORMATION

The angel of transformation resembles a beautiful butterfly with the radiant colours of spring flowers, the rising sun and calm blue sky. This angel is magnificent, radiant and scintillating and filled with beauty. She uses her light to shine on new projects and thus strengthen and encourage us to bring angelic energy into our practical everyday tasks. She is also the angel of new projects.

The angel says:

'It is helpful to think of the life cycle of a butterfly, which goes through four stages: the egg, the caterpillar, the chrysalis and the butterfly. Whatever your projects are, they will be in one of these stages. Even when your project appears to be finished there will either be another one or a renewal of a part of the project.

'The egg stage is the beginning of everything. An idea is born but not yet reality. Is it just a thought or an idea?

'The caterpillar stage is when you decide to start to create your project in the world. Do you need to make a decision?

'The cocoon stage is when you "go within"'to meditate and decide what you are going to do. What are you doing to make the idea reality?'

'The butterfly is born from the chrysalis. It is the birth stage. Are you sharing your ideas and projects with others?'

and fertility, as is Gabriel.

The *air* initiation is concerned with the mastery of our thoughts. How often have you lain awake at night, with your thoughts seemingly going round and round to torment you and prevent sleep from coming? When you are worried or fearful, your breath is tense and shallow. Breath (air) is very closely connected with our thoughts and we can use the breath and Archangel Raphael to help us to master the negative thoughts that torment us in our darkest moments.

Slow, deep breathing takes control of the mind and helps us to become calmer. Blow the breath out through the lips until your lungs are as empty as possible. Wait for the impulse of the breath to breathe in again. Call on Raphael to help you breathe deeply and slowly when lying awake at night with worrying thoughts, or when undergoing a stressful time.

The *fire* initiation brings the warmth of love, enthusiasm and passion into life. We learn to find things that we enjoy doing and feel enthusiastic about. There can be no life without the sun and the spiritual sun within and behind it, so the angel of fire, Archangel Uriel, stands with us as we endeavour to feel warmth and enthusiasm about the things we need to do. Imagine you are breathing in orange fire and light to find courage and energy and the enthusiasm for what needs to be done. Uriel helps you to find your *joie de vivre* once again, to find clarity.

The *earth* initiation enables us to realize that all living things, sentient beings, plants, rocks and minerals and the stars and planets of the universe, are all part of the Source, all contain the living, divine energy of life. Archangel Michael stands beside us as we strive to remember and overcome all our fears. He lends us his sword of truth and justice until we find our way again. It is the sword, which protects and guides everyone, through the great crises in their lives.

The element of ether, working through all of the six senses and higher dimensions, supports us through all of the initiations we undergo.

ACTIVITY: BUTTERFLIES!

If you like being creative, doodle, draw, colour or paint butterflies! Do an Internet search about butterflies and find free clip art pictures you can print or copy for inspiration. Write a creative story or poem about butterflies and transformation. If you are very artistic, paint the butterfly angel, the angel of transformation.

WITH THE ANGEL OF TRANSFORMATION

Hear the angel: 'In your own life, you may be in one of the transformative stages. You may be going through what appears to be darkness. Like the caterpillar hatching from the egg or the butterfly emerging from the chrysalis, be confident that you are safe and cared for. Life is a never-ending cycle of transformation. Birth or rebirth is painful. I will help you if you call on me when you know it's time for change, either in relationships or career. I will help you to break out of your restrictions, your chrysalis.

'You might be going through a major life-change. If you feel you are in too much of a hurry or can't get everything done, call on me. Maybe you need to relax and be less serious. I will always help you.

'I will be with you when you notice the colours you are drawn to. I will remind you what they mean. If you want to break a bad habit, decide on a plan to change it and call on the butterfly angel. When you can, meander around a park or garden or a wild place and observe butterflies in their natural surroundings. Notice what your thoughts were when you suddenly saw one, then meditate on the meaning and purpose. Use natural movement dance, with drumming or music, either by yourself or with others.'

A FINAL MESSAGE FROM THE DEVAS

In spite of the worry about the environment, we would fill you with hope, for the tide of carelessness has turned to caring. The universe works with the law of attraction. If people are fearful, fear is attracted. Believe that thoughts attract what you really want to happen. All the angels, devas and nature spirits need you to create what you really want for planet Earth and they will help us and multiply the results.

HOPE

The tide has turned
In spite of those who would fill you with
despair about Gaia,
Our beautiful planet,
We would fill you with HOPE!
WE see that the tide of carelessness
Towards the environment
Has turned to CARING.
Find the positive messages in the news.
Tune in to the law of positive attraction
For all aspects of life are subject to a law of
attraction.
Belief in attracting what you really want
the Planet to respond to
Is the secret to bringing into reality
the results that Gaia, the devas

and the elementals
Also desire.
Co-operation with us will multiply and
bring the results
We all visualize.

Live joyfully
So life is filled with
JOY and ENJOYMENT,
Meaning 'Joy is meant.'

Live in THANKS
So your life is full of Thankfulness

Live hopefully
So your life is filled with HOPE.

THANK YOU

DEFINITIONS

ANGEL: a supernatural being who mediates between God (the Supreme Creator) and human beings. Angels minister over all living things and the natural world. The term angel is derived from the Greek word 'angelos,' meaning messenger. (ENCYCLOPAEDIA OF ANGELS, Rosemary Ellen Guiley)

ARCHANGEL: a higher order of Angels in the hierarchy: a group of Archangels who stand above the others and higher than all the other angelic orders regardless of their place in the hierarchy. (ANGELS A–Z, Matthew Bunsen.)

DEVA: an advanced spirit or god-being who governs the elementals and the well-being of all things in nature. (ENCYCLOPAEDIA OF ANGELS, Rosemary Ellen Guiley). In Sanskrit, the word 'deva' means Shining One. In the New Age movement, 'deva' implies spiritual forces or beings behind nature (Wikipedia.) In some New Age thinking, a deva is thought of as an angel, nature spirit or fairy.

ELEMENTAL: a lower order of spirit being that exists as the life force in the natural world. They are said to govern minerals, plants and animals; the four elements of earth, air, fire and water. They are ruled by Angels. (ENCYCLOPAEDIA OF ANGELS, Rosemary Ellen Guiley)

FAIRIES: nature spirits who tend growing things; they are the elemental entities of and Earth, Air, Fire and Water.

NOTES

Page 13

[1]Currently, left/right brain function is considered more complex.

[2]Sperry, R.W. 'Hemisphere Disconnection and Unity in Conscious Awareness.' *American Psychologist 23* (1968), pp. 723-3

Page 14

[1]see 'Do women and men have different brains?', article by Gina Rippon, a cognitive neuroscientist, in *The New Scientist*, 2 March 2019, p. 18

Page 17

[1]For further reading on these subjects, see Lothrop, Anya, ZENTANGLE ART THERAPY (www.gmcbooks.com) and Summers, Olivia, ZENDOODLE: THE MASTERY SERIES (Success Life Publishing)

Page 21

[1]Andrews, Ted. ENCHANTMENT OF THE FAERIE REALM. Llewellyn Publications, Minnesota, 1994

Page 33

[1]See Pert, Candace B., EVERYTHING YOU NEED TO KNOW TO FEEL GOOD (Hay House, 2006) and Lipton, Bruce, THE BIOLOGY OF BELIEF (Cygnus Books, 2005)

Page 35

[1]Andrews, Ted. ENCHANTMENT OF THE FAERIE REALM. Llewellyn Publications, Minnesota, 1994

Page 38

[1]Unpublished White Eagle teaching © copyright White Eagle Lodge

[2]White Eagle, SPIRITUAL UNFOLDMENT I (White Eagle Lodge, 1961)

Page 39

[1]See my book, ESSENTIAL OILS AND MEDITATION, London, Polair, 2007 p. 9.

Page 49

[1]See www.YouTube: 'Elephants mourning Lawrence Anthony

Page 68

[1]Carey, Kenneth, THE RETURN OF THE BIRD TRIBES (Harper Collins, 1991)

Page 72

[1]White Eagle reference

Page 76

[1]Godwin, Malcolm. ANGELS: AN ENDANGERED SPECIES, (Boxtree, 1993)

Page 78

[1]Lamborn Wilson, Peter. ANGELS (Thames and Hudson, 1980)

Page 83

White Eagle, WHITE EAGLE ON FESTIVALS AND CELEBRATIONS (White Eagle Lodge, 2003)

Page 84
[1]For more information, see 'The Healing Herbs of Edward Bach' by Julian and Martine Barnard)

Page 85
[1]*Evening Standard*, March 18th, 2019
[2]Wikipedia: The Great Pacific Garbage Patch

[3]*Positive News*, March 20th, 2019

Page 89
[1]From *Stella Polaris* magazine, June-July, 1961

Page 91
[1]INITIATIONS ON THE PATH OF THE SOUL, White Eagle, 2007

LIST OF ILLUSTRATIONS

Illustrations by Patrick Gamble
The frontispiece painting (p. 2) is entitled 'The Tree where Dreams Began'; the one on p. 48 is called 'The Tree of Twin Souls'. On p. 90, the title for the painting is 'Harmony', and on p. 98 it is 'Sacred Place'. The cover painting is called 'The Spirit Tree'.

Illustrations by Bodel Rikys
Bodel has contributed the drawings on pp. 3 and 73, 'Fire Sprites', on p. 36, 'Music Sprites', and on p. 97, 'Butterfly Fairy'.
Photographs not by the author include those on p. 81 (by Anna Hayward). Commercial images are acknowledged *in situ*.

LIST OF MESSAGES FROM ANGELS AND DEVAS

ACTIVITIES, MEDITATIONS AND EXERCISES

SUBJECT INDEX

DEVAS AND NATURE SPIRITS
AND HOW TO COMMUNICATE WITH THEM